HOW TO IDENTIFY
MUSHROOMS
TO GENUS IV:

HOW TO IDENTIFY MUSHROOMS TO GENUS IV:
Keys to Families and Genera

BY DANIEL E. STUNTZ

Editorial changes by
David L. Largent and Roy Watling

Daniel E. Stuntz
Department of Botany
Univ. of Washington
Seattle, Washington

David L. Largent
Biology Department
Humboldt State Univ.
Arcata, California
95521

Roy Watling
Royal Botanic Garden
Inverleith Row
Edinburgh, Scotland
EH3 LR5

© David L. Largent

Published by: Mad River Press, Inc.
Route 2 Box 151-B
Eureka, California 95501

Printed by: Eureka Printing Co., Inc.
Eureka, California 95501

ISBN #0-916-422-10-0

Anyone who begins to study the "modern" system of classifying agarics soon realizes that Singer's book is perplexing to use but phenomenally informative. Since these keys are published in order to make Singer's system more understandable, we thought it would be appropriate to dedicate this volume to him.

TABLE OF CONTENTS

INTRODUCTION AND PREFACE

While completing my doctorate at the University of Washington, I was able to use and obtain copies of three separate keys to the genera of mushrooms devised by Daniel E. Stuntz.

The first key was a key to the genera of mushrooms recognized by Elias Fries; such genera are commonly called the Friesian Genera. This key has been published at the end of "How to Identify Mushrooms to Genus I: Macroscopic Features."

The second key relates the Friesian Genera given in the first key to the genera recognized by Singer in the third edition of the "Agaricales in Modern Taxonomy." As far as I'm aware, there is only one other key similar to this one—namely the key found on pages 2-30 of Kühner and Romagnesi's "Flore Analytique des Champignons Superieurs." Stuntz's key allows the student of agarics not only to begin to understand the bewildering array of new agaric names but also to get some idea of the historical changes that have occurred in the Friesian Genera. This key is for all practical purposes the same as that originally constructed by Stuntz except the page numbers following each genus refer to Singer's third edition. Consequently, several genera in Singer's newest book may have been omitted.

The third key devised by Stuntz is one which allows the student in agarics to identify the families, tribes and genera of agarics recognized by Singer in his third edition. Stuntz and most other agaricologists found Singer's keys extremely difficult to use, not because of any inaccuracies but more so because of the length of each key choice. This difficulty made use of Singer's exceptional book very cumbersome and tended to make all of us very frustrated. Particularly frustrating was the fact that Singer's book contained all the information required to understand contemporary agaricology. Consequently, Stuntz proceeded to put all of the characteristics of each of the genera recognized by Singer onto Unisort cards. Afterwhich, he chose features or combinations of features that were less cumbersome than in Singer's book and formulated a key. Unfortunately, Stuntz's original key was to Singer's second edition. In order to publish this key, the genera, families and tribes had to be "updated" to correspond to Singer's third edition—thus the contributions of Roy Watling and myself. Since Roy and I are far more self-centered than Daniel, we had to (unfortunately) make some change in the taxonomic scheme outlined by Singer. Such changes are indicated as appending notes at the end of the respective families. I sincerely doubt that such changes detract from Stuntz's original purpose for a few similar changes exist in Daniel's original key. For completeness, family descriptions have been added by one of us (R.W.).

2

With the publication of these keys, two things have been accomplished. Firstly, students of agarics now have considerable flexibility in their approach to agaricology. They can key a mushroom to a Friesian genus using the first key which stresses macroscopic features. Then they can key a segregate genus from the Friesian genus using the second key which requires a knowledge of microscopic features. Or, if they so choose, they can key the segregate genus out directly using the third key which involves a combination of micro- and macroscopic features. Secondly, a dream has come true for me. Ever since I knew of these keys by Daniel Stuntz, I thought they should be published. The amount of effort put forth in their construction is incomprehensible to most people; the usefulness of the keys is unbelieveable. With their publication, I now know that the study of agarics will be enhanced.

David L. Largent
Eureka, California
August, 1977.

Key I

RELATION OF FRIESIAN GENERA
TO SINGER'S CLASSIFICATION

In the following section of the agaric key, the Friesian genera found in "How to Identify Mushrooms Vol. I" are arranged in alphabetical order, and the current status of each genus is given. If the genus has the same circumscription today as it had originally, it is designated as "unchanged", but if its species are now classified in one or more segregate genera, a key to these genera is provided. The modern scheme of classification presented is that adopted by R. Singer, and numbers in parentheses following generic names refer to pages in his "Agaricales in Modern Taxonomy" (third edition).

Agaricus
(=Psalliota)

1. Pileal surface an epithelium, and spore print at first green or olive-green, becoming purplish brown upon drying ....**Melanophyllum** (466)

1. Pileal surface not an epithelium; or if it is one (in some tropical species), then the spore print is purple-brown or chocolate brown from the first, never green ....**Agaricus** (459)

Amanita

Unchanged, except for the inclusion by most present-day mycologists of **Vaginata** (=**Amanitopsis**). E.-J. Gilbert has proposed that **Amanita** be subdivided into the genera given in the key below. Even the French mycologists, however, have not accepted his proposal, although some of them (e. g., Kühner & Romagnesi) use the taxa as subgenera of **Amanita**.

1. Spores amyloid 2

1. Spores inamyloid 6

    2. Spores spherical or very short-ellipsoid; volva sheathing, sack-like .... **Amanitina**

    2. Spores ellipsoid to elongate-ellipsoid or cylindrical; nature of the volva varies 3

3. Volva membranous, sack-like, or at least strongly sheathing, and with a conspicuous free margin 4

3. Volva friable, leaving warts or scales on the pileal surface and on the base of the stipe, never sack-like or sheathing 5

4. Annulus powdery or mealy-floccose; spores elongate-ellipsoid; sporocarps often bruising red or brown .... **Amidella**

4. Annulus membranous; spores short-ellipsoid; sporocarps not bruising red or brown .... **Amanitina**

5(3). Annulus membranous, ample; stipe without floccose scales below the annulus .... **Amplariella**

5. Annulus mealy or floccose-powdery; stipe with floccose scales below the annulus .... **Aspidella**

6(1). Annulus lacking altogether; spores spherical ...... **Amanitopsis**

6. Annulus present; spores ellipsoidal 7

7. Volva membranous, ample, sack-like, with conspicuous free limb; pileal surface not covered with warts; base of stipe not bulbous .... **Amanita**

7. Volva friable, closely appressed to the bulbous base of the stipe, with a slight free limb, or merely forming warts on the base of the stipe; pileal surface covered wth warts (velar remnants) .... **Amanitaria**

Amanitopsis

See **Vaginata**.

Annularia

See **Chamaeota**.

Armillaria

Some present-day agaricologists abandon this genus altogether, assigning all of its species to the genera other than **Armillaria** given in the key below: others retain a genus **Armillaria**, the circumscription of which varies with each mycologist. The scheme of partition given below is that advocated by Singer.

1. Pileal surface an epithelium .... **Cystoderma** (478)

1. Pileal surface not an epithelium 2

2. Base of the stipe with a large, marginate bulb, connected to the margin of the young pileus by a well developed cortina, as in the section **Bulbopodium** of **Cortinarius;** spores pale ochraceous in mass .... **Leucocortinarius** (624)

2. Base of the stipe not marginate-bulbous; partial veil not a cortina; spores usually white in mass, may be cream-color or pallid yellowish 3

3. Spores amyloid; lamellar trama divergent 4

3. Spores inamyloid; lamellar trama parallel, subparallel, or interwoven, rarely slightly divergent 5

4. Lamellae long-decurrent; veil double, forming two annuli on the stipe; spores oblong to ellipsoid-cylindric ... **Catathelasma** (298)

4. Lamellae adnexed to emarginate, not decurrent; veil not double, forming only one annulus on the stipe; spores ellipsoid to short-ellipsoid .... **Armillaria** (299)

5(3). Pileal surface a glutinous cuticle consisting of a hymeniform layer superimposed upon a thick gelatinous stratum; spores, basidia, and cystidia extremely large, the spores spherical or nearly so .... **Oudemansiella** (344)

5. Pileal surface not constituted as in the above (it may, however, be viscid); spores and basidia of "normal size", cystidia rarely present, and then not extremely large 6

6. Lamellae decurrent, at least by a tooth; black rhizomorphs associated with the sporocarps; lamellar trama of young sporocarps often slightly divergent .... **Armillariella** (259)

6. Lamellae not decurrent; no black rhizomorphs associated with the sporocarps; lamellar trama of young sporocarps never divergent . 7

7. Stipe eccentric; spores cylindrical; lamellar trama very irregular (interwoven), with prominent subhymenium .... **Pleurotus** (181)

7. Stipe central; spores subglobose to ellipsoidal; lamellar trama regular (parallel) or nearly so 8

8. Basidia with carminophilous granulation; hyphae with clamps; spores echinulate .... **Calocybe** (223)

8. Basidia without carminophilous granulation; clamps not present; spores smooth .... **Tricholoma** (251)

Asterophora
(=Nyctalis)

Unchanged.

Bolbitius

Unchanged, except that most agaricologists now include **Pluteolus** in **Bolbitius**.

Boletus

The genus **Boletus** has been considerably changed by many present-day mycologists as Fries' genus covered all soft putrescent poroid fungi. Several boletoid genera are found only in the tropics and were not covered by the old classifications. **Strobilomyces** and **Porphyrellus** are even taken out of **Boletus** and placed in a family separate from that containing the majority of species.

1. Spore-print lemon-yellow, vinaceous to clay-pink, 'purple-brown' (vinaceous brown) or 'purple-black' (fuscous black) 2

1. Spore-print with distinct ochraceous, cinnamon, rust or olivaceous tints, never lemon-yellow, vinaceous to clay-pink, 'purple-brown' or 'purple-black' 5

  2. Spore-print lemon-yellow or vinaceous to clay-pink 3

  2. Spore-print 'purple-black' (fuscous black) or 'purple-brown' (vinaceous brown) 4

3. Spore-print lemon-yellow; spores ellipsoid in side- and face-views .... **Gyroporus**

3. Spore-print vinaceous to clay-pink; spores subfusiform in side-view .... **Tylopilus**

  4(2). Spore-print 'purple-brown' (vinaceous brown); spores subfusiform in side-view, smooth .... **Porphyrellus**

  4. Spore-print 'purple-black' (fuscous black); spores subglobose - globose, distinctly ornamented .... **Strobilomyces**

5(1). Hymenium on anastomosing, subporiform, angular pores ....
                                          ......**Xerocomus** pro parte

5. Hymenium on the inner surface of distinct tubes 6

6. Spores ellipsoid in face- and side-views; tubes very short and difficult to separate from pileus flesh .... **Gyrodon**

6. Spores subfusiform in side-view or, if ellipsoid, longer than 6 um or tubes red; tubes variable in length and easily separable from pileus flesh 7

7. Pileus typically glutinous or viscid, more rarely humid, never dry; cystidia within tubes either in bundles with golden or brownish incrustations or large and filled with yellow juice 8

7. Pileus rarely glutinous, usually humid or dry, at most greasy-viscid in wet weather; cystidia if present in tubes irregular, clavate, fusiform or lageniform, lacking coloured incrustations or bright yellow sap, and rarely if ever aggregated into bundles 9

8. Cystidia especially those at and approaching tube-mouths large, filled with yellow sap, not aggregated into fascicles; stipe striate-fibrillose infrequently minutely punctate at apex; lacking ring; tubes bright lemon-chrome; in broadleaved woods ...... **Pulveroboletus**

8. Cystidia at tube-mouths and within tubes usually aggregated into bundles and often covered in coloured amorphous incrustations; stipe with or without ring often glandular punctate at least at apex; tubes ochraceous rust, olivaceous sepia, lemon-yellow or greyish; in conifer woods .... **Suillus** pro parte

9(7). Pileus felty-scaly; tubes deeply decurrent and stipe sheathed in white ring; spore-print olivaceous yellow to almost citrine ....
.... **Suillus** pro parte

9. Pileus smooth to wrinkled, humid, rarely if ever felty or scaly; stem without ring and tubes adnate, uncinate or free, less frequently truly decurrent; spore-print infrequently olivaceous yellow and never when tubes are decurrent 10

10(9). Stipe roughened or wooly floccose with coloured or colourless scabrosities which usually darken with age; spore-print ochreous to snuff-brown without olivaceous tints; spores 15 um or larger, rarely less than 13 um .... **Leccinum**

10. Stipe punctate, veined-reticulate or +/− smooth, less frequently rugulose or ribbed and lacking darkening floccose scabrosities although frequently punctate with brownish or coloured dots; spore-print either with distinct olivaceous flush not distinctly rust-colour; spores various, often less than 15 um long 11

11. Hymenophoral trama with lateral stratum consisting of slightly divergent hyphae touching each other and not strongly curved outwards, often becoming rather irregular in age and only paler (if at all) from the mediostratum; tubes angular and wide often sublamellate .... **Xerocomus**

11. Hymenophoral trama with lateral stratum consisting of loosely arranged hyphae curving outwards and generally less pigmented than the mediostratum; tubes narrow to sometimes wide but never gill-like .... **Boletus**

Cantharellus

Not now considered a member of the Agaricales. Some authors (e.g., Smith and Morse, Mycologia 39, 1947) retain **Cantharellus** in the Friesian sense except for a few species that they consider to be Clitocybes; others recognize one or more of the segregate genera given in the key below.

1. Spores angular-tuberculate; context black or purplish black, becoming green in dilute KOH .... **Polyozellus** (798)

1. Spores not angular-tuberculate; context not black or purplish black, and not turning green in KOH 2

2. Spores amyloid or dextrinoid 3

2. Spores inamyloid (and not dextrinoid) 4

3. Spores amyloid; lamellae white or pallid .... **Cantharellula** (284)

3. Spores dextrinoid; lamellae orange or yellow (rarely white) ......
...... **Hygrophoropsis** (497)

4(2). Sporocarps growing on living mosses ...... **Leptoglossum** (279)

4. Sporocarps not growing on living mosses 5

5. Spores yellow or ochraceous; spore wall wrinkled or warted or otherwise roughened .... **Gomphus** (588)

5. Spores white to yellow, spore wall smooth 6

6. Dextrinoid metuloids present in the hymenium; metuloids also strongly metachromatic in cresyl blue .... **Geopetalum** (193)

6. Metuloids lacking .... **Cantharellus** (788)

Chamaeota
(=Annularia)

Unchanged.

Claudopus
(see **Entolomataceae**, Key II)

1. Spores angular (as seen in any view) .... **Rhodophyllus** (672)
1. Spores smooth, entire, cylindrical to allantoid ... **Phyllotopsis** (180)

Clitocybe

H. E. Bigelow, the North American specialist in **Clitocybe**, defines the genus very nearly in the Friesian sense, also placing in it most of the species commonly referred to **Omphalina.** The more narrow circumscription of **Clitocybe** favored by Singer and many other agaricologists is indicated in the following key.

1. Spores either amyloid or dextrinoid 2
1. Spores neither amyloid nor dextrinoid 4

  2. Lamellae regularly dichotomously forked 3
  2. Lamellae not dichotomously forked; spores amyloid ....
                   .....**Leucopaxillus** (291)

3. Spores dextrinoid; lamellae strongly colored (yellow or orange) ......
                   .....**Hygrophoropsis** (688)
3. Spores amyloid; lamellae white or pallid cream- to rose-tinged ......
                   .....**Cantharellula** (284)

  4(1). Edge of the lamellae with abundant, large, conspicuous cheilocystidia .... **Tricholomopsis** (249)
  4. Edge of lamellae lacking cheilocystidia, or at most with small, inconspicuous ones 5

5. Spores spiny or rough-walled 6
5. Spores smooth 8

  6. Spores pink or vinaceous-fawn in mass .... **Lepista** (245)
  6. Spores white 7

7. Lamellae thick and waxy-appearing, with broad, regular trama; spores large, globose or broadly ellipsoidal, conspicuously spiny .....
...... **Laccaria** (230)

7. Lamellae thin, the trama not notably broad; spores small (4-6u diam), finely roughened ("punctate") .... **Clitocybe** (234)

8(5). Lamellae thick and waxy-appearing, with broad, regular trama; spores oblong, large (11-22u long) .... **Laccaria** (230)

8. Lamellae thin (or at least not notably thick), the trama not notably broad; spores not as in the above 9

9. Clamps present 10

9. Clamps lacking .... **Armillariella** (259)

10. Basidia with carminophilous granulation ...... **Lyophyllum** (218)

10. Basidia not with carminophilous granulation 11

11. Sporocarps lignicolous, strongly pigmented (orange, yellow-orange); spores small, globose .... **Omphalotus** (232)

11. Not with the above combination of characteristics . **Clitocybe** (234)

Clitopilus

1. Spores angular as seen in any view .... **Rhodophyllus** (672)

1. Spores angular (or ridged, or notched) only as seen in end-view, appearing smooth or merely striated in lateral view 2

2. Spores rough-walled, granular or warty .... **Rhodocybe** (669)

2. Spores appearing longitudinally striate (because of longitudinally oriented grooves or ridges) .... **Clitopilus** (667)

Collybia

In the key below are included most of the genera to which Singer assigns species originally described as Collybias; I have left out a few in which he places only one or two tropical species. Many contemporary agaricologists (e.g., A.H. Smith, Kühner & Romagnesi) use a broader concept of **Collybia** than does Singer. The genus always has been—and remains—difficult to delimit in a satisfactory manner.

1. Spores amyloid 2

1. Spores inamyloid 3

    2. Cuticular layers of the pileus well differentiated from the under-lying pileal trama, often with scattered pileocystidia; spores very small, less than 5u in their longest dimension .... **Baeospora** (409)

    2. Cuticular layers not well differentiated from the underlying pileal trama; spores 5u or more in their largest dimension ....
    ......**Clitocybula** (288)

3(1). Edge of lamellae heteromorphous from abundant cheilocystidia; habitat lignicolous; pileal surface composed of repent hyphae that are often tipped with cystidioid elements .... **Tricholomopsis** (249)

3. Not with the above combination of characteristics 4

    4. Pileal surface well differentiated, hymeniform or cellular, or con-sisting of a trichodermium or ixotrichodermium, with or without gelatinized layers or pileocystidia 5

    4. Pileal surface undifferentiated, or at most a cutis of repent hyphae, which may or may not be diverticulate 12

5. Clamps present; habitat varies 7

5. Clamps absent; sporocarps growing on cones of conifers, or of **Magnolia** 6

    6. Hymenophoral trama bilateral .... **Pseudohiatula** (415)

    6. Hymenophoral trama regular .... **Strobilurus** (549)

    7. Pileal surface a cutis, of diverticulate hyphae ...... **Collybia** (308)

    7. Pileal surface cellular, hymeniform, a trichodermium, or with viscid or gelatinized layers 8

8. Pileus dry 9

8. Pileus viscid 11

9. Pileus and stipe covered with bright chrome yellow, mealy floccae (consisting of vesiculose elements; i.e., pileal surface essentially an epithelium that becomes fragmented) .... **Cyptotrama** (416)

9. Pileus and stipe not covered with bright yellow, mealy floccae 10

10. Pileal surface a trichodermium; stipe deeply radicating; spores 9-12 x 6-7u or larger; large pleurocystidia (60-85u long) present in the hymenium; tramal hyphae inamyloid .... **Oudemansiella** (344)

10. Pileal surface cellular or hymeniform; stipe not radicating; spores and cystidia (if present) smaller than the above; tramal hyphae distinctly dextrinoid .... **Marasmius** (350)

11(8). Sporocarps lignicolous; pileal surface an ixotrichodermium, with projecting pileocystidia; spores 5-8 x 2-3u; stipe not radicating (except that it may extend into cracks in the wood) .... **Flammulina** (413)

11. Terrestrial (or perhaps in some instances growing from deeply buried wood); pileal surface a humenial layer superimposed upon a gelatinized layer; spores 8-12 x 6-8u or larger; stipe deeply radicating the ground .... **Oudemansiella** (413)

12(4). Clamps present 13

12. Clamps lacking 16

13. Spore wall roughened, or punctate with imbedded spinules, or spiny 14

13. Spore wall smooth 15

14. Basidia with carminophilous granulation ...... **Lyophyllum** (218)

14. Basidia without carminophilous granulation .... **Fayodia** (404)

15(13). Basidia with carminophilous granulation ..... **Lyophyllum** (218)

15. Basidia without carminophilous granulation .... **Collybia** (308)

16(12). Spores (and often also the basidia) of dried specimens containing purplish to vinaceous granules when examined in dilute KOH; sporocarps colored .... **Callistosporium** (270)

16. Spores (and basidia) of dried specimens lacking purplish or vinaceous granules when examined in KOH; sporocarps lacking pigmentation (white or nearly so) .... **Podabrella** (276)

Coprinus

Unchanged by some agaricologists; by others, divided as follows:

1. Lamellae deliquescing .... **Coprinus** (496)
1. Lamellae not deliquescing .... **Pseudocoprinus** (497)

Cortinarius

Left intact by most present-day agaricologists (A.H. Smith, Singer, Kühner & Romagnesi, Orton), but M. Moser, one of the principal European specialists in the genus, subdivides it as follows (note that Singer regards Moser's genera as subgenera):

1. Pileus viscid 2
1. Pileus not viscid 3

   2. Stipe slimy-viscid .... **Myxacium** (603)
   2. Stipe not viscid .... **Phlegmacium** (591)

3(1). Pileus hygrophanous 4
3. Pileus not hygrophanous 5

   4. Yellow pigments predominating, and spores globose to subglobose .... **Cortinarius** (620)
   4. Yellow pigments not predominating; or if they do predominate, then the spores are ellipsoidal or amygdaliform .. **Telamonia** (607)

5(3). Pileus squarrose-scaly or revolute-scaly 6
5. Pileus silky-smooth, or innately fibrillose, or appressed-scaly 7

   6. Young lamellae bluish, pale violet, or pallid .... **Phlegmacium,** subgenus **Sericeocybe** (602)
   6. Young lamellae yellow, olive-green, olive-brown, or dark violet .... **Cortinarius** (620)

7(5). Young lamellae bluish, pale violaceous, or pallid .... **Phlegmacium,** subgenus **Sericeocybe** (613)
7. Young lamellae colored otherwise .... **Dermocybe** (620), also **Leprocybe**-stirps **Orellani** (618)

Crepidotus

1. Spores purplish or fuscous violet in mass, with an apical germ-pore; pileal surface more or less viscid, consisting of broad, repent hyphae .... **Melanotus** (543)

1. Spores chamois, or some shade of brown or rusty brown, with or without apical germ-pore; pileal surface not viscid, varying in its structure 2

   2. Spores with ornamented walls 3

   2. Spores smooth-walled 4

3. Spores bright rusty brown or orange-brown in mass, their wall warted or granular; tramal hyphae with abundant water-soluble, bright yellow pigment .... **Pyrrhoglossum** (628)

3. Spores clay-colored to cinnamon brown in mass, their wall punctate-appearing from imbedded spinules; tramal hyphae lacking bright yellow, water-soluble pigment .... **Crepidotus** (653)

   4(2). Clamps present 5

   4. Clamps lacking 9

5. Pileal surface a palisade-trichodermium, the terminal cells of which are frequently cystidioid 6

5. Pileal surface a cutis (layer of repent hyphae) 7

   6. Spores dull brown, or grayish brown, or umber in mass; cells of the trichodermium not incrusted with pigment .... **Simocybe** (651)

   6. Spores red-brown to yellow-brown in mass; cells of the tricho-dermium incrusted with fulvous or rufous pigment ....**Phaeomarasmius** (561)

7(5). Spores with an apical germ-pore .... **Pleuroflammula** (560)

7. Spores without an apical germ-pore 8

8. Spores an intense olivaceous-umber to a deep rusty brown in mass; veil present on young specimens; bright yellow, water-soluble pigments present in the tramal hyphae of many species . . . . **Pleuroflammula** (560)

8. Spores clay-color to cinnamon brown in mass; veil absent in young specimens; tramal hyphae never having bright yellow, water-soluble pigment . . . . **Crepidotus** (653)

9(4). Spores buff to chamois or, pinkish chamois in mass . . . . **Pleurotellus** (658)

9. Spores clay-color, cinnamon brown, or rusty brown in mass . . . . **Crepidotus** (653)

Eccilia

Sometimes included in **Rhodophyllus** (often as a subgenus); more often than not excluded as a genus.

Entoloma

Sometimes included in **Rhodophyllus** (often as a subgenus). See Entolomataceae, Key II.

Flammula

Flammula sensu Fries was a heterogeneous collection of brown-spores agarics, very difficult to delimit in any satisfactory manner, especially with respect to **Pholiota**. Current practice eliminates it, relegating most of its species to a subgenus of **Pholiota**, and relocating the remainder as indicated in the following key:

1. Spores punctate-roughened to spinulose or warted 2

1. Spores smooth 3

2. Pileus strongly colored, blackening in 10% KOH, not viscid; spores bright rusty brown or orange-brown in mass, amygdaliform or inequilaterally ellipsoidal in outline; sporocarps lignicolous . . . . **Gymnopilus** (625)

2. Pileus pallid, viscid, not blackening in strong KOH; spores grayish yellow-brown in mass, globose-subangular; sporocarps terrestrial . . . . **Ripartites** (692)

3(1). Spores brownish olivaceous in mass, boletoid in outline; lamellae bright chrome yellow, with divergent trama .. **Phylloporus** (717)

3. Spores lacking any olivaceous or greenish tints in mass, and not boletoid in outline; lamellae neither bright chrome yellow, nor with divergent trama 4

    4. Pileus viscid . . . . subgenus **Flammula**
                                                      of **Pholiota** (551)

    4. Pileus not viscid 5

5. Spores subreniform . . . . **Inocybe** (569)

5. Spores ellipsoidal to inequilaterally amygdaliform . . . . subgenus **Flammula** of **Pholiota** (551)

Galera

Galera is unavailable as a generic name in the fungi, having been used in 1825 for a genus of orchids. Most agaricologists now divide its species between the two genera **Galerina** and **Conocybe**, but some follow Singer in the more elaborate scheme of segregate genera shown below.

1. Pileal surface cellular or hymeniform; spores with a definite apical germ-pore 2

1. Pileal surface a cutis of repent hyphae; spores without a germ-pore, or at most with a very small, narrow one . . . . **Galerina** (629)

    2. Lamellar trama with well developed mediostratum; pileus never plicate-sulcate; cheilocystidia rarely subcapitate . **Pholiotina** (518)

    2. Lamellar trama consisting mainly of the two broad bands of hymenopodium, the mediostratum very much reduced; pileus plicate-sulcate, or if it is not so, then the cheilocystidia are abruptly capitate 3

3. Pileus plicate-sulcate; cheilocystidia ampullaceous, not capitate . . . . . .
                                                       . . . . . . **Galerella** (518)

3. Pileus smooth (sometimes translucent-striate when wet); cheilocystidia abruptly capitate . . . . **Conocybe** (514)

Gomphidius

1. Universal veil (as seen on the pileal surface and on the stipe) consisting of sphaerocytes .... **Cystogomphus** (695)

1. Universal veil not consisting of sphaerocytes 2

    2. At least a zone of the pileal trama amyloid; mycelium at base of stipe of young sporocarps amyloid, and having large clamp connections .... **Chroogomphus** (698)

    2. Pileal trama either inamyloid, or at most dextrinoid; mycelium at base of stipe of young sporocarps inamyloid ... **Gomphidius** (695)

Hebeloma

Unchanged.

Hygrophorus

Several present-day agaricologists (e.g., Smith & Hesler; Dennis, Orton and Hora) retain the genus in the original Friesian sense. The European mycologists have a tendency to consider as genera the classical subgenera **Limacium, Hygrocybe,** and **Camophyllus**. Singer, who goes furthest in subdividing **Hygrophorus**, recognizes the following segregate genera:

1. Spores stellate-echinate, with subcylindric to elongate-conic spines ...
      ...... **Hygroaster** (200)

1. Spores smooth (unornamented) 2

    2. Spores amyloid .... **Neohygrophorus** (206)

    2. Spores inamyloid 3

3. Pileal surface hymeniform, or a palisade of swollen cells ....
      ...... **Aeruginospora** (204)

3. Pileal surface never hymeniform or cellular 4

    4. Clamps present 5

    4. Clamps absent 7

5. Pileal surface a viscid pellicle; lamellar trama divergent ....
..... **Hygrophorus** (197)

5. Pileal surface viscid or not viscid, but lamellar trama parallel or interwoven, not divergent 6

6. Lamellar trama strongly interwoven .... **Camarophyllus** (204)

6. Lamellar trama parallel to subparallel .... **Hygrocybe** (207)

7(4). Sporocarps with bright pigments (red, yellow, orange, etc.); lamellae not decurrent .... **Humidocutis** (211)

7. Sporocarps with dull-colored pigments (brown, fuscous, gray, dull green, etc.), or none (hence white); lamellae decurrent ....
..... **Aeruginospora** (204)

Hypholoma

In this instance, nomenclature seems to cause more trouble than taxonomy, the problem being what generic name to use for the taxon called **Psathyrella** in the key below. A.H. Smith, in his most recent mimeographed key to Agaricales, calls it **Hypholoma**, Singer (1962) continues to call it **Psathyrella**, and Kühner & Romagnesi use the invalid generic name **Drosophila** Quélet. All seem agreed as to the delimitation of the two taxa concerned.

1. Pileal surface hymeniform or cellular; chrysocystidia lacking (but other kinds of cystidia may be present) .... **Psathyrella** (497)

1. Pileal surface a cutis of repent hyphae, often underlain by a more or less cellular hypoderm (hence caution in sectioning is necessary, not to be misled by tearing off the cuticular layer); chrysocystidia present .... **Naematoloma** (533)

Inocybe

Unchanged, except that from time to time, a few agaricologists have tried (unsuccessfully) to revive Britzelmayr's genus **Clypeus** (syn.: **Astrosporina** Schröter) for the Inocybes with nodulose or spiny spores.

Lactarius

Unchanged.

Lentinus

The key given below represents Singer's idea of how the species of **Lentinus** sensu Fries and ss. Saccardo should be reclassified. Several of his contemporaries, though recognizing **Lentinellus**, leave the remainder of the species in **Lentinus**, which thus retains essentially its original delimitation.

1. Spores amyloid .... **Lentinellus** (794)
1. Spores inamyloid 2

  2. Sporocarp arising from a large, hard sclerotium . **Pleurotus** (304)
  2. Sporocarp not arising from a sclerotium 3

3. Spores ellipsoidal to subglobose 4
3. Spores cylindrical or fusoid (elongated) 5

  4. Lamellar trama parallel to subparallel, or at least parallel in an axial zone (the mediostratum); edge of the lamellae serrate ....
       ...... **Lentinus** (189)

  4. Lamellar trama interwoven, with no mediostratum present; edge of the lamellae entire .... **Nothopanus** (304)

5(3). Lamellar trama parallel to subparallel, or at least with parallel hyphae forming a mediostratum .... **Lentinus** (189)
5. Lamellar trama interwoven, lacking a mediostratum of parallel or subparallel hyphae 6

  6. Subhymenium very well developed .... **Pleurotus** (304)
  6. Subhymenium very scantily developed, or practically absent .....
      ...... **Panus** (185)

Lepiota

The segregate genera in the following key are those recognized by Singer. Many mycologists (e.g., A.H. Smith; Dennis, Orton, & Hora) recognize only **Limacella** and **Leucocoprinus**, assigning to the latter either all Lepiotas with dextrinoid spores and apical germ-pore, or only those that are thin-fleshed and sulcate-striate.

1. Lamellar trama divergent 2
1. Lamellar trama not divergent 3

    2. Pileus (and often also the stipe) viscid; spores white or cream-color in mass; stipe not radicating; sporocarps not arising from the nests of termites .... **Limacella** (430)

    2. Pileus and stipe not viscid; spores pink in mass; stipe radicating deeply, with a long "taproot"; sporocarps arising from the nests of termites .... **Termitomyces** (277)

3(1). Spore-print blue-green at first, becoming purplish as it dries; pileal surface an epithelium, becoming deeply powdery from dissociated sphaerocysts .... **Melanophyllum** (466)

3. Not with the above combination of characteristics 4

    4. Spores either dextrinoid or amyloid 5
    4. Spores neither dextrinoid nor amyloid 11

5. Spore print green .... **Chlorophyllum** (447)

5. Spore print white, pale pink, yellowish, or ochraceous cream, never green 6

    6. Spores amyloid .... **Lepiota** (472)

    6. Spores dextrinoid 7

7. Pileal trama amyloid; Pileal surface of repent hyphae ....
            ...... **Pseudobaeospora** (476)

7. Pileal trama inamyloid; pileal surface varies, but is rarely of repent hyphae 8

    8. Spores having an apical germ-pore, and metachromatic in cresyl blue 9

    8. Spores neither having a germ-pore, nor metachromatic in cresyl blue .... **Lepiota** (472)

9. Clamps present (use the velar tissue; i.e., the annulus) ....
           ...... **Macrolepiota** (449)

9. Clamps lacking 10

10. Pileus very thin-fleshed, consequently becoming long-sulcate or plicate-striate; stipe usually considerably longer than the diameter of the pileus; inflated "pseudoparaphyses" common or numerous in the hymenium .... **Leucocoprinus** (449)

10. Pileus thick and fleshy, not long-sulcate or plicate-striate; stipe rarely much longer than the diameter of the pileus; inflated "pseudoparaphyses" absent, or at least uncommon ....
...... **Leucoagaricus** (451)

11(4). Pileus surface a thin layer of heteromerous tissue (i.e., a mixture of sphaerocysts and filamentous hyphae); all parts of the sporocarp lacking pigments .... **Smithiomyces** (470)

11. Pileal surface hymeniform or cellular; at least some part of the sporocarp pigmented 12

12. Pileal surface a single layer of isodiametric cells; pileal trama weakly dextrinoid .... **Cystolepiota** (471)

12. Pileal surface hymeniform, of pedicellate, subclavate cells, not isodiametric ones; pileal trama neither dextrinoid nor amyloid ....
...... **Chamaemyces** (469)

Leptonia

Sometimes included in **Rhodophyllus** (often as a subgenus). See Entolomatacene, Key II.

Marasmius

The delimitation of **Marasmius** with respect to **Collybia** and to certain sections of **Mycena** never has been easy, and still is not. Singer recognizes several genera in the Marasmius-complex, as shown in the following key (which seems also to indicate a certain difficulty in delimitation of two of the segregate genera, **Marasmiellus** and **Mycenella**). A.H. Smith, and Kühner, recognize **Crinipellis** and **Xeromphalina**, but include the species of **Micromphale** and **Marasmiellus** in **Marasmius**.

1. Spores amyloid; stipe with a tuft of fulvous hairs at its base ....
...... **Xeromphalina** (407)

1. Spores inamyloid; base of stipe with or without hairs, which are variously colored if present 2

2. Cells of the pileal surface layers dextrinoid 3

2. Cells of the pileal surface layers not dextrinoid 4

3. Cuticular elements in the form of long, more or less thick-walled hairs, or of slender, flagellar outgrowths from a disk-like cell ....
...... **Crinipellis** (368)

3. Cuticular elements not long hairs or flagellar outgrowths ....
...... **Marasmius** (350)

4(2). Pileal surface hymenform or cellular 5

4. Pileal surface or repent hyphae that may be smooth, encrusted, or diverticulate 9

5. Pileal surface with broom-cells .... **Marasmius** (350)

5. Pileal surface lacking broom-cells 6

6. Spores spiny, or otherwise ornamented ...... **Mycenella** (346)

6. Spores smooth 7

7. Context of pileus and stipe dextrinoid (or rarely amyloid) ....
...... **Marasmius** (350)

7. Context of pileus and stipe inamyloid (and never dextrinoid) 8

8. Spores globose to subglobose .... **Mycenella** (346)

8. Spores not globose to subglobose .... **Marasmius** (350)

9(4). Spores globose or nearly so 10

9. Spores not globose or subglobose 11

10. Pleurocystidia present .... **Mycenella** (346)

10. Pleurocystidia lacking .... **Collybia** (307)

11(9). Tramal hyphae of pileus and stipe at least in part dextrinoid; spores oblong, clavate, fusiform, or elongatelunate . **Marasmius** (350)

11. All tramal hyphae (pileus and stipe) inamyloid, and not dextrinoid; spores varying in shape, but rarely, if ever, clavate or lunate 12

12. Spores angular to stellate-nodulose .... **Marasmiellus** (315)

12. Spores neither angular nor stellate-nodulose 13

Mycena

The two recognized authorities on **Mycena**, A.H. Smith and R. Kühner, both accept the genus in very nearly its original Friesian limits: i.e., they do not recognize segregate genera on the basis of amyloidity, epicuticular structure, and other more or less correlated characteristics. Singer, on the other hand, does recognize segregate genera on such bases, as is shown in the following key:

1. Stipe when cut exuding either a colorless, watery juice, or a white or colored juice 2

1. Stipe not exuding any juice when cut 3

    2. Juice colorless, like water; spores inamyloid ..... **Hydropus** (397)

    2. Juice white or colored; spores sometimes inamyloid, but more frequently weakly to strongly amyloid .... **Mycena** (384)

3(1). Spores amyloid 4

3. Spores inamyloid 7

    4. Spores globose, appearing minutely punctate because of fine pores or canals in the (inamyloid) middle layer of the spore wall ...
    ...... **Fayodia** (404)

    4. Spores varying in shape, but with smooth, unornamented, one layered wall 5

5. Surface of pileus covered with a veil composed of large, thick-walled cells, overlying the thin epicutis which is composed of slender, thinwalled hyphae; sporocarps very small, lacking pigment, the hymenophore venose to sublamellate .... **Delicatula** (383)

5. Surface of pileus without a veil, or if one is present, it is not composed of thickwalled cells; stature of the sporocarps varies, but they are frequently pigmented, and the hymenophore is distinctly lamellate . 6

6. Cuticular elements of pileal surface diverticulate, or smooth, inflated, and hyaline, or the pileus (and often also the stipe) viscid .. .. **Mycena** (384)

6. Epicuticular elements never diverticulate, often inflated but then pigmented; neither pileus nor stipe viscid .... **Hydropus** (397)

7(3). Spores spiny, or finely punctate 8

7. Spores smooth, unornamented 9

8. Spores globose, spiny, or with rod-like projections .... **Mycenella** (346)

8. Spores ellipsoid, appearing finely punctate because of minute perforations in the spore wall .... **Fayodia** (404)

9(7). Spores globose, with large, very conspicuous hilar appendage .... **Mycenella** (346)

9. Spores short-ellipsoid to cylindric or fusoid, lacking a conspicuous hilar appendage 10

10. Cells of the trama with clamps; habitat varies 11

10. Tramal elements lacking clamps; habitat on ferns, or on cones ... . **Pseudohiatula** (415)

11. Cells of pileal surface diverticulate, or surface pilose; pigments lacking .... **Hemimycena** (380)

11. Cells of pileal surface smooth, or the surface corticated (of swollen cells); surface cells with fuscous pigment .... **Hydropus** (397)

Naucoria

Since the 1870's, **Naucoria** sensu Fries has been recognized as being an artificial grouping of unrelated species. Of the segregate genera split off from it, almost all present-day agaricologists recognize **Agrocybe** and **Phaeocollybia**, but opinions are divided as to the validity of the remainder. A.H. Smith recognizes **Agrocybe**, **Kuehneromyces**, **Alnicola**, and **Phaeocollybia**, and makes **Phaeomarasmius** a subgenus of **Naucoria**. Kühner & Romagnesi accept **Agrocybe** and **Phaeocollybia**, combining the remaining genera in one genus **Naucoria**. Almost every mycologist concerned with the agarics has a different way of dealing with the problem; Singer's solution is given in the key below. Notice that he does not, for nomenclatural reasons (see p. 798 of "Agaricales"), use the name **Naucoria**.

1. Spores ornamented (punctate-roughened to warted) 2
1. Spores smooth 3

   2. Pileal surface a viscid pellicle (of decumbent hyphae, in mature specimens); stipe deeply radicating, for a distance usually much longer than the part above ground; associated with a variety of trees (mostly conifers), but not specifically with alder ....
      ..... **Phaeocollybia** (638)

   2. Pileal surface dry or hygrophanous, not viscid, the cuticular hyphae with cystidioid terminal cells, or mixed with sphaerocysts; stipe not radicating; sporocarps associated (apparently constantly) with alder .... **Alnicola** (582)

3 (1). Spores having an evident apical germ-pore 4
3. Spores either lacking a germ-pore altogether, or with a very inconspicuous one (difficult to see clearly), or with a callus 5

   4. Pileal surface hymeniform .... **Agrocybe** (523)
   4. Pileal surface of repent hyphae .... **Kuehneromyces** (555)

5 (3). Pileal surface hymeniform, composed of globose to pyriform pedicellate cells .... **Agrocybe** (523)
5. Pileal surface a palisade-trichodermium or an epithelium 6

   6. Clamp connections present 7
   6. Clamps absent .... **Simocybe** (651)

7. Spores ochraceous, yellow-brown, or rusty brown in mass; cells of pileal surface encrusted with crystals or pigment; pileal surface punctate-scaly or floccose-scaly .... **Phaeomarasmius** (561)
7. Spores dull fuscous brown or olivaceous umber in mass; cells of pileal surface not encrusted; pileal surface glabrous or nearly so ....
     ..... **Simocybe** (651)

Nolanea

Sometimes included in **Rhodophyllus**, sometimes as a subgenus. See Entolomataceae, Key 1.

Nyctalis

See **Asterophora**.

Omphalia

See **Omphalina**.

Omphalina
(=Omphalia)

Some agaricologists still recognize **Omphalina** in essentially the Friesian sense; others (e.g., H.E. Bigelow, A.H. Smith) include its species in **Clitocybe**. According to Singer, species of **Omphalina** ss. Fries should be distributed among the following thirteen genera:

1. Spores amyloid 2
1. Spores inamyloid 10

  2. Tramal hyphae of stipe or pileus, or both, amyloid or dextrinoid ...
                                 ...... **Mycena** (384)
  2. Tramal hyphae of stipe and pileus inamyloid (and not dextrinoid) ..
                                   3

3. Pileus at first covered with a veil that is composed of thickwalled cells, and is underlain by a thin cutis of thinwalled, parallel hyphae; hymenophore venose or sublamellate .... **Delicatula** (383)
3. Pileus lacking a veil of thickwalled cells; pileal surface varies; hymenophore definitely lamellate 4

  4. Pileal surface either an epicutis of repent, smooth, non-diverticulate hyphae, or a viscid pellicle 5
  4. Pileal surface cellular or hymeniform, or composed of diverticulate hyphae .... **Mycena** (384)

5. Pileus viscid 6
5. Pileus not viscid 7

6. Sporocarps with one or more of the following characteristics: . . . . .
. . . . . . **Mycena** (384)

    a) Pigments lacking, or if present, bright colored
    b) Subhymenium gelatinous
    c) Edge of lamellae gelatinized
    d) Cellular hypoderm well developed
    e) Context of pileus or stipe (or both) amyloid or dextrinoid

6. Sporocarps not having any of the above characteristics . . . .
. . . . . . **Fayodia** (404)

7(5). Stipe tough, corneous, bearing a tuft of fulvous hairs at its base . . .
. . . . . . **Xeromphalina** (407)

7. Stipe not notably tough, with hyaline hairs, or no hairs, at its base . 8

    8. Cheilocystidia numerous, often conspicuous; pleurocystidia often
    present . . . . **Mycena** (384)

    8. Cheilocystidia few and inconspicuous, or lacking; pleurocystidia
    absent 9

9. Sporocarps lignicolous; pigments gray or fuliginous, neither incrusting
nor membranal . . . . **Clitocybula** (288)

9. Sporocarps terrestrial (or growing on charcoal); pigments ochre, clay
color, or deep cinnamon, incrusting . . . . **Pseudoomphalina** (286)

    10(1). Spores appearing finely punctate because of minute cylindrical
    perforations in the spore wall . . . . **Fayodia** (404)

    10. Spores smooth 11

11. Stipe exuding a watery juice when cut; pileus corticate, the surface
broad cells containing a fuscous-olivaceous pigment . . **Hydropus** (397)

11. Stipe not exuding a watery juice; pileus corticate or not 12

    12. Pileal surface of diverticulate hyphae, or containing conspicuous
    pilose elements, or corticate, or having a well developed subcellular
    hypoderm underlying a thin cutis of smooth, parallel hyphae . . . 13

    12. Pileal surface of repent, radial, smooth-walled hyphae, often little
    differentiated from the underlying pileal context, and never with
    the other characteristics mentioned above 15

13. Sporocarps having one or more of the following features: ....
...... **Mycena** (384)
   a) Well developed cellular hypoderm
   b) Cortical hyphae of stipe metachromatic in cresyl blue
   c) Any part of the trama amyloid or dextrinoid
   d) Lamellar trama of parallel hyphae
   e) Cheilocystidia clavate, with diverticulate apex
   f) Base of stipe insititious

13. Sporocarps with none of the above characteristics 14

   14. Lamellar trama of interwoven hyphae that are either slightly
   gelatinized or densely compacted; pigments none, or very scanty
   (sporocarps white or nearly so) .... **Hemimycena** (380)

   14. Lamellar trama regular to subregular, and neither gelatinized nor
   densely compacted; pigments present (sporocarps colored) ......
   ...... **Neoclitocybe** (313)

15 (12). Clamps present 16

15. Clamps lacking 19

   16. Basidia with carminophilous granulation ...... **Lyophyllum** (218)

   16. Basidia without carminophilous granulation 17

17. Lamellar trama parallel or nearly so; pileus hygrophanous; pigments,
   if present, not incrusting .... **Clitocybe** (234)

17. Lamellar trama interwoven (but there may be a narrow sub-parallel
   mediostratum); other characteristics varying 18

   18. Pigments incrusting the hyphae .... **Omphalina** (263)

   18. Pigments absent, or if present, intracellular .... **Gerronema** (265)

19 (15). Pigment lacking, or if present, intracellular ... **Gerronema** (265)

19. Pigments present, incrusting the hyphae 20

   20. Hymenophore venose or sublamellate .... **Leptoglossum** (279)

   20. Hymenophore distinctly lamellate .... **Omphalina** (263)

Panaeolus

For many present-day agaricologists (e.g., A.H. Smith, Kühner, Romagnesi) this genus remains as Fries delimited it, except for the inclusion of **Psilocybe foenisecii**. Singer advocates the following segregate genera:

1. Spores warted .... **Panaeolina** (506)
1. Spores smooth 2

2. Pleurocystidia present 3
2. Pleurocystidia absent .... **Panaeolus** (507)

3. Pleurocystidia thickwalled, colored (melleous), with acute apex; context of pileus and stipe becoming blue where exposed or bruised .. .. **Copelandia** (509)
3. Pleurocystidia thinwalled, of the chrysocystidium-type; context not becoming blue where exposed or bruised 4

4. Pileus viscid, pallid or pale ochraceous .... **Annellaria** (510)
4. Pileus not viscid, very dark colored, almost black . **Panaeolus** (507)

Panus

The delimitation of **Panus, Pleurotus**, and **Lentinus** proposed by Singer (see key below), based mainly on tramal characteristics, is not accepted by everyone. Kühner & Romagnesi, as well as A.H. Smith, separate these genera on the basis of the marcescent nature of the pileal tissues, and the serrate or entire edge of the lamellae, rather than on the basis of lamellar trama. They do, however, recognize certain segregate genera (**Panellus, Lentinellus** on the basis of amyloidity of the spores. **Panus** is considered synonymous with **Lentinus** by one of us (R.W.).

1. Spores amyloid; pileus laterally attached, sessile, or at most with a short lateral stipe 2
1. Spores inamyloid; attachment of pileus varies 3

2. Spores strongly amyloid; pellicular veil absent .... **Panellus** (339)
2. Spores weakly amyloid; pellicular veil present, covering the lamellae in young specimens .... **Tectella** (337)

3 (1). Sporocarps sessile, or at most with a short lateral stipe 4

3. Sporocarps stipitate, stipe central to eccentric 7

    4. Pileal surface a layer of dichophysate hyphae .... **Asterotus** (331)

    4. Pileal surface layers not containing dichophysate hyphae 5

5. Lamellae covered in young specimens with a pellicular veil ....
                              ...... **Tectella** (337)

5. Pellicular veil lacking 6

    6. Spores cylindric .... **Panus** (185)

    6. Spores subglobose to ellipsoidal .... **Nothopanus** (304)

7 (3). Spores subglobose to ellipsoidal, never ellipsoid-oblong or cylin-dric-allantoid; pileus thin and membranous .... **Nothopanus** (304)

7. Spores oblong to cylindric or fusoid or allantoid; pileus not thin and membranous 8

    8. Lamellar trama parallel or subparallel, or at least with strong axial arrangement; clamps absent, or very few .... **Lentinus** (189)

    8. Lamellar trama interwoven, not even with any axial arrangement; clamps present, numerous 9

9. Subhymenium well developed, conspicuous, often separating from the lamellar trama in alkaline mounts, with pressure .... **Pleurotus** (181)

9. Subhymenium very much reduced, or absent .... **Panus** (185)

Paxillus

Paxillus is another of the Friesian genera that became eventually so heterogeneous that Fries himself was moved to comment (in Hymenomycetes Europaei) that it was "poorly defined." The relocation of its original species indicated in the following key is now universally accepted.

1. Spores with ornamented or sculptured wall 2

1. Spores smooth 4

2. Coscinoids and coscinocystidia present; lamellar trama divergent; sporocarps with red pigment (strictly tropical genus) ....
...... **Linderomyces** (795)

2. Neither coscinoids nor coscinocystidia present; lamellar trama not divergent; sporocarps lacking red pigment (north-temperate and south-temperate genera) 3

3. Spores sordid pink or pinkish cream in mass .... **Lepista** (245)

3. Spores grayish ochraceous brown in mass .... **Ripartites** (483)

4 (1). Spores boletoid; pileal surface becoming bright blue in vapors of ammonia (in young, fresh specimens); lamellae bright lemon yellow or chrome yellow .... **Phylloporus** (717)

4. Spores ellipsoid; pileal surface not turning bright blue in ammonia vapors; lamellae never bright lemon or chrome yellow . **Paxillus** (689)

Pholiota

The majority of contemporary agaricologists include the smooth-spored species of **Flammula** (sensu Fries) in the residual genus **Pholiota**, after having removed from **Pholiota** sensu Fries a number of discrepant elements, as shown in the key below.

1. Spores smooth 2

1. Spores ornamented; surface varying from finely punctate-roughened to distinctly warted 12

2. Pileus, lower part of the stipe, and lower surface of the large, flaring annulus, all covered with an epithelium that makes these surfaces mealy or powdery; spores ochraceous in mass ....
...... **Phaeolepiota** (481)

2. Neither pileus nor stipe with an epithelium; pileal surface varies from a trichodermium to a cutis of repent or fasciculate hyphae, or a viscid pellicle; spores some shade of brown in mass (darker than ochraceous) 3

3. Pileal surface glabrous, either hymeniform or a cellular layer 1 to 2 cells deep; spores with an evident apical germ-pore 4

3. Pileal surface not hymeniform or cellular (but it may be glabrous); spores with or without an apical germ-pore 5

4. Spores bright rusty brown or orange-brown in mass; sporocarps small, fragile, mycenoid, with slender (ca. 1-3 mm), fragile or brittle stipe .... **Pholiotina** (518)

(often included in **Conocybe**)

4. Spores dark brown, burnt umber or chocolate color in mass; sporocarps medium-sized to large, with clitocyboid or tricholomatoid aspect, the stipe fleshy and stout .... **Agrocybe** (523)

5 (3). Spores with conspicuous germ-pore that makes the apex of the spore look truncate; pileus glabrous and hygrophanous, neither viscid nor scaly .... **Kuehneromyces** (555)

5. Spores lacking an apical germ-pore altogether, or if one is present, it is inconspicuous and difficult to demonstrate, and never makes the apex of the spore look truncate; pileus frequently (but not always!) viscid or scaly 6

6. Pileus viscid .... **Pholiota** (546)

6. Pileus not viscid 7

7. Pileus scaly 8

7. Pileus not scaly 11

8. Pleurocystidia of some sort (metuloids, leptocystidia, chrysocystidia) present .... **Pholiota** (546)

8. Pleurocystidia lacking (but cheilocystidia are usually present) .. 9

9. Scales formed by the fasciculation of a palisade-trichodermium that is composed of short, rather broad, incrusted cells; spores bright or rich rusty brown in mass, with very thick, double wall ....

...... **Phaeomarasmius** (561)

9. Scales formed from fascicles of agglutinated hyphae whose cells are cylindrical, not derived from a palisade-trichodermium; spores dull cinnamon brown or dull umber in mass, the wall often double, but not notably thick 10

10. Basidiocarps lignicolous .... **Pholiota** (546)

10. Basidiocarps terrestrial .... **Inocybe** (569)

11 (7). Pileal surface a cutis of repent, radial, more or less parallel hyphae .... **Pholiota** (546)

11. Pileal surface a palisade-trichodermium, composed of chains of short, broad cells .... **Phaeomarasmius** (561)

12 (1). Pileus viscid 13

12. Pileus not viscid 14

13. Pleurocystidia absent; pileus thick and fleshy; sporocarps terrestrial, with deeply radicating stipe .... **Hebeloma** (577)

13. Pleurocystidia present; pileus thin, submembranous; sporocarps lignicolous; stipe not radicating .... **Galerina** (629)

  14 (12). Pileal surface an epithelium (which is also present on the stipe and lower surface of the annulus); only a few of the spores slightly punctate; spore print ochraceous ..... **Phaeolepiota** (481)

  14. Pileal surface not an epithelium; all mature spores ornamented; spore-print bright rusty brown or orange-brown 15

15. Spores with a suprahilar smooth plage; pleurocystidia present, projecting beyond the hymenium (i.e., notably longer than the basidia); sporocarps mostly lignicolous, and the pileus not blackening in 10% KOH; if terrestrial, the base of the stipe lacks volva-like membranous patches .... **Galernia** (629)

15. Spores lacking a smooth suprahilar plage; pleurocystidia absent, or if present, not longer than the basidia, and hence not projecting beyond hymenium; if the sporocarps are lignicolous, their surface blackens in 10% KOH; if terrestrial, the base of the stipe has volva-like membranous patches or rings 16

  16. Sporocarps terrestrial; base of the stipe with volva-like membranous patches or appressed rings, the same velar material giving the pileal surface a white "sheen"; pileal surface not blackening in 10% KOH; spores with a rather conspicuous apical callus; cheilocystidia scattered and inconspicuous, the edge of the lamellae not heteromorphous .... **Rozites** (586)

  16. Sporocarps lignicolous; base of stipe lacking velar remnants in the form of volva-like patches; pileal surface blackening in 10% KOH; spores lacking an apical callus; cheilocystidia numerous, making the edge of the lamellae heteromorphous .... **Gymnopilus** (625)

Pleurotus

As can be seen by the fact that Singer distributes its species among 21 genera, **Pleurotus** sensu Fries had by the latter part of the nineteenth century become simply a dumping-ground for all the white-spored or nearly-white-spored agarics with pleurotoid habit that were not readily assignable to **Panus, Lentinus, Tricholoma,** or **Clitocybe.** The Singerian dismemberment of **Pleurotus** is not as violent as it seems at first, however, since several of the segregate genera contain only one species, or very few species, or are strongly localized in distribution (mostly tropical), and an additional number are generally accepted genera (e.g., **Tricholomopsis**) that are not, strictly speaking, segregates of **Pleurotus,** but are genera to which pleurotoid species had been wrongly assigned. Contemporary mycologists are not in agreement as to which of the Singerian pleurotoid genera should be considered valid, but few of them any longer accept **Pleurotus** in its original Friesian delimitation.

1. Spores amyloid or dextrinoid 2
1. Spores neither amyloid nor dextrinoid 4

   2. Spores dextrinoid; pileal surface bearing thickwalled, elongated, dextrinoid hairs . . . . **Chaetocalathus** (371)

   2. Spores amyloid; pileal surface without thickwalled, dextrinoid hairs
   3

3. Spores globose to broadly ellipsoidal; some part of the trama usually amyloid, none of it gelatinized . . . . **Lentinellus** (794)

3. Spores cylindrical to allantoid, narrow, small (ca. 3u long); no part of the trama amyloid or dextrinoid, but some part of it gelatinized . . . . .
   . . . . . . **Panellus** (339)

   4(1). Pileal surface covered with thickwalled, elongated, strongly dextrinoid hairs . . . . **Chaetocalathus** (371)

   4. Pileal surface often fibrillose or shaggy or tomentose, but the hairs not dextrinoid 5

5. Lamellae strongly colored, cinnabar at first becoming purple then black, or black from the first; tissues of the hymenophore with abundant black granules that form a blue-green solution in KOH . . . . .
   . . . . . . **Anthracophyllum** (307)

5. Lamellae if colored, not as in the above; tissue of the hymenophore without black granules that become blue-green in KOH 6

6. Pileal surface a hymeniform layer of vesiculose or ampullaceous, thickwalled cells, underlain by a gelatinized zone; lamellar trama of young specimens decidedly divergent; spores pink in mass, punctate-roughened .... **Rhodotus** (418)

6. Not with the above combination of characteristics 7

7. Spores pink in mass, cylindric to allantoid, small; pileal surface covered with a dense, sponge-like, hygrophanous tomentum .... **Phyllotopsis** (180)

7. Not with the above combination of characteristics 8

8. Clamps present 9

8. Clamps absent 10

9. Spore-print pure white; spores very small (3u diam), globose .... **Pleurocollybia** (274)

9. Spore-print "cream buff" to "chamois" spores larger than the above, (ca. 6 x 3u), ellipsoidal .... **Pleurotellus** (658)

10(8). Sporocarp (mostly the lamellae) strongly luminescent; spores globose, very large (13-17u diam) .... **Lampteromyces** (232)

10. Sporocarp not luminescent; spores if globose not as large as in the above 11

11. Edge of the lamellae with abundant, voluminous, conspicuous cheilocystidia, which often have yellow content or walls .... **Tricholomopsis** (249)

11. Edge of lamellae with or without cheilocystidia, but when these are present they are relatively small and inconspicuous, or are slender and filamentous 12

12. Pileal trama (sometimes also the hymenophoral trama) with gelatinized layers or areas 13

12. None of the trama gelatinized 14

13. Large, thickwalled, conspicuous metuloids present in the hymenium ..... **Hohenbuehelia** (332)

13. No metuloids present in the hymenium .... **Resupinatus** (330)

14(12). Sporocarps growing attached to living mosses, or among mosses on rotten wood .... **Leptoglossum** (279)

14. Sporocarps not attached to moss plants; growing on wood (but then not among mosses), or rarely on the ground 15

15. Edge of the lamellae serrate, denticulate, or crenulate, in mature specimens .... see **Lentinus** (189)

15. Edge of lamellae entire (smooth) in mature specimens 16

    16. Sporocarps terrestrial .... **Gerronema** (265)

    16. Sporocarps lignicolous 17

17. Pileal surface a trichodermium; spores globose to globose-subangular ...... **Cheimonophyllum** (306)

17. Not with the above combination of characteristics 18

    18. Spores cylindric; lamellar trama interwoven, with conspicuous and voluminous subhymenium .... **Pleurotus** (181)

    18. Spores globose to ellipsodial, never cylindric; lamellar trama varies, but lacks a conspicuous subhymenium 19

19. Lamellar trama parallel or subparallel; sporocarps stipitate, with thick-fleshed, fibrous pileus 20

19. Lamellar trama interwoven; sporocarps sessile, or attached by a lateral "pseudostipe" or tubercle, the pileus thin-fleshed, almost membranous 21

    20. Basidia with carminophilous granulation ...... **Lyophyllum** (209)

    20. Basidia without carminophilous granulation .... **Hypsizygus** (240)

21(19). Pileus tough and pliable; lamellae subdistant to distant; tropical species .... **Nothopanus** (308)

21. Pileus soft and fleshy; lamellae close; species of temperate regions .. .. **Pleurocybella** (now=Nothopanus)

Pluteolus

Usually included in **Bolbitius**, often as a subgenus; if accepted as an autonomous genus, unchanged from the Friesian sense.

Pluteus

Unchanged.

Psalliota

See **Agaricus.**

Psathyra

Now considered a synonym of **Psathyrella.** Kühner & Romagnesi make it a subgenus of the genus **Drosophila** Quélet (an invalid generic name).

Psathyrella

In the original Friesian sense, this was a tribe of black-spored agarics, but it also contained some species with purple-brown spores. Some of the black-spored species (e.g., **Agaricus disseminatus**), with certain plicate-striate Coprini whose lamellae do not deliquesce, comprise the genus **Pseudocoprinus** Kühner, recognized by A.H. Smith, but now reduced to synonymy with **Coprinus** by Kühner himself, and by Singer. If, after excluding from **Psathyrella** the Pseudocoprini, a purple-brown-spored species is chosen as lectotype, **Psathyrella** becomes a genus of purple-brown-spored agarics, and then can assimilate the species of **Psathyra**, which must be discarded in any case, as it is a later homonym of a genus of seed plants. In this emended sense, **Psathyrella** is accepted by most present-day agaricologists, the only question being that of deciding which of several generic names is the correct one.

Psilocybe

1. Pileal surface cellular 2

1. Pileal surface a cutis of filamentous hyphae (often underlain by a sub-cellular hypoderm), or a viscid pellicle 3

    2. Spores with warted walls .... **Panaeolina** (506)

    2. Spores with smooth walls .... **Psathyrella** (497)

38

3(1). Chrysocystidia present; subcellular hypoderm usually well
developed .... **Naematoloma** (533)

3. Chrysocystidia absent; subcellular hypoderm absent, or poorly
developed .... **Psilocybe** (536)

Russula

Unchanged.

Schizophyllum

Unchanged.

Stropharia

1. Pileal surface cellular .... **Psathyrella** (497)
1. Pileal surface not cellular 2

2. Context becoming blue or greenish blue where exposed or bruised
...... **Psilocybe** (536)
2. Context not bluing upon exposure or bruising ... **Stropharia** (530)

Tricholoma

Most of the genera given in the key below are accepted by
contemporary mycologists: the possible exceptions are **Dermoloma**,
Porpoloma, **Rhodocybe**, and **Calocybe**. **Dennisomyces** is found (thus far)
only in the American tropics. **Rhodopaxillus** often has been used instead
of **Lepista** for "Tricholomas" with pink, rough-walled spores, but it is a
later homonym.

1. Spores amyloid 2
1. Spores inamyloid 7

2. Spores ornamented (punctate-roughened to warted) 3
2. Spores smooth 4

3. Clamps present; spores with a smooth suprahilar plage; pleurocystidia absent .... **Leucopaxillus** (291)

3. Clamps absent; spores with a smooth suprahilar plage; pleurocystidia often (but not always) present .... **Melanoleuca** (294)

4(2). Pileal surface a palisade of inflated, isodiametric, or stalked-clavate cells .... **Dermoloma** (402)

4. Pileal surface a cutis of filamentous, interwoven or parallel hyphae, sometimes with pileocystidia, but never hymeniform 5

5. Pleurocystidia present (only tropical species known) ....
..... **Dennisomyces** (401)

5. Pleurocystidia absent (both tropical and temperate-region species known) 6

6. Spores strongly amyloid .... **Porpoloma** (290)

6. Spores very slightly amyloid .... **Leucopaxillus** (291)

7(1). Pileal surface cellular, or hymeniform, or consisting of sphaerocysts
..... 8

7. Pileal surface an interwoven or parallel filamentous hyphae, or forming a cartilaginous cortical layer 9

8. Basidia with carminophilous granulation .... **Calocybe** (223)

8. Basidia without carminophilous granulation ..... **Dermoloma** (402)

9(7). Spore print pale pink, salmon-color, ochraceous salmon, or grayish violaceous 10

9. Spore print white to cream-color or pale ochraceous, lacking any pink or violaceous tones 12

10. Spores smooth in lateral view, but angular to rounded-angular in end-view .... **Rhodocybe** (669)

10. Spores rough-walled (punctate-roughened to warted) 11

11. Clamps present .... **Lepista** (245)

11. Clamps absent .... **Rhodocybe** (669)

12(9). Partial veil a distinct, often voluminous, cortina 13

12. Partial veil (if present) not a cortina 14

13. Clamps present; stipe with a large marginate-bulbous base; spores very thickwalled, ochraceous in print . . . . **Leucortinarius** (624)

13. Clamps lacking; stipe not conspicuously marginate-bulbed; spores neither very thickwalled, nor ochraceous in print . . **Tricholoma** (251)

14(12). Clamps present 15

14. Clamps lacking . . . . **Tricholoma** (251)

15. Edge of the lamelae heteromorphous with voluminous, conspicuous cheilocystidia; sporocarps lignicolous . . . . **Tricholomopsis** (249)

15. Edge of lamellae without cheilocystidia, or if present, they are neither conspicuous nor voluminous; sporocarps not lignicolous . . . 16

16. Basidia with carminophilous granulation 17

16. Basidia without carminophilous granulation . . . . **Tricholoma** (251)

17. Sporocarps white, or nearly so 18

17. Sporocarps pigmented (colored, not white) 19

18. Basidia not more than 20 mcr long; spores small, 4-6 x 3 mcr . . . . .
. . . . . . **Calocybe** (223)

18. Basidia more than 20 mcr long; spores larger than the above . . . .
. . . . . . **Lyophyllum** (218)

19(17). Having one or more of the following features: . **Lyophyllum** (218)
    a) Pigments dull colored (gray, sordid brown, etc.)
    b) Context becoming black or bluish black where bruised
    c) Spores angular or triangular or angular-nodulose

19. Not having any of the features listed above (pigments bright colored; yellow, fulvous, blue, pink, violet, etc.) . . . . **Calocybe** (223)

Trogia

Fries based this genus on a tropical species, **Cantharellus aplorutis** Montagne, that has a centrally stipitate sporocarp with infundibuliform pileus and venose hymenophore. Later he included the boreal fungus now known as **Plicatura crispa**, and since the mycologists of temperate regions were acquainted with **Plicatura** and not with Montagne's "**Cantharellus**," **Trogia** for them meant a sessile merulioid fungus rather than a stipitate, cantharelloid one. It is in this incorrect sense that Kauffman and many others used the generic name **Trogia**, although

Patouillard in 1900 had pointed out the error of doing so.

1. Sporocarp stipitate, infundibuliform, the stipe arising from a conspicuous "pedestal" or "socket"; spores ellipsoid . . . . **Trogia** (523)
1. Sporocarp sessile and laterally attached, or effusoreflexed, more or less dimidiate or conchoid; spores cylindric . . . . **Plicatura** (798)

Tubaria

1. Spores purple-brown, with thick walls and apical germ-pore . . . .
. . . . . . **Psilocybe** (536)
1. Spores light ferruginous brown, thinwalled, without apical germ-pore
. . . . . . **Tubaria** (647)

Vaginata
(=Amanitopsis)

Unchanged, if considered an autonomous genus; otherwise included in **Amanita**.

Volvaria

See **Volvariella**.

Volvariella
(=Volvaria)

Unchanged.

KEY II
GENERA ACCEPTED IN
MODERN CLASSIFICATION OF AGARICS

This section of the agaric key is concerned with most of the genera currently recognized by agaricologists. It is not a key to the entire assemblage of taxa included in Agaricales sensu Singer, since most of Singer's "reduced series" (i.e. genera without lamellate hymenophore) and the Polyporaceae sensu strictior have for the most part been omitted. Numbers in parentheses following a generic name refer to the page in the third edition (1975) of Singer's "Agaricales in Modern Taxonomy" on which a description of the genus is given. The circumscription of families and tribes is not necessarily the same in this key as it is in Singer's book.

The key is based primarily on histochemical reactions and anatomical features, such things as lamellar attachment, velar structures, etc., being used only as a last resort. Consequently, it usually will be necessary to have the following data, particularly if the agaric is white-spored:

1. Presence or absence of clamps
2. Reaction of any part (especially the spores!) with Melzer's reagent
3. Shape and ornamentation of the spore
4. Presence or lack of an apical germ pore
5. Exact color of the spore print
6. Structure of the pileal surface
7. Structure of the lamellar trama

A key to families is given first, after which the families are taken in alphabetical order, with a short diagnosis, and a key to their genera.

KEY TO FAMILIES

1. Pileus trama heteromerous .... Russulaceae
1. Pileus trama homoiomerous, if containing swollen cells never heteromerous 2

   2. Hymenophoral trama bilateral or divergent 3
   2. Hymenophoral trama convergent (inverse) or regular to irregular .
            11

3. Spores black in mass (olivaceous, fuscous or violaceous black) 4
3. Spores white to cream or flushed greenish or greyish, or some shade of brown to yellow, or pinkish 5

   4. Spores ornamented, globose to ellipsoid; hymenophore poroid or lamellate .... Strobilomycetaceae
   4. Spores smooth, boletiform; hymenophore lamellate ....
             ...... Gomphidiaceae

5(3). Spores yelllow to white 6
5. Spores some shade of brown 8

   6. Spores yellow, ellipsoid; hyphae in stipe arranged annularly ......
             ...... Boletaceae
   6. Spores white, varying from globose or subglobose to bacciliform; hyphae in stipe aligned with axis of stipe 7

   7. Large elements of hymenophoral trama composed of rather swollen units; velar remnants very evident .... Amanitaceae
   7. Elements of hymenophoral trama filamentous or at most swollen in outer layer of lateral stratum only; velar remnants rarely evident ...
             ...... Tricholomataceae

   8(5). Hymenophore lamellate .... Paxillaceae
   8. Hymenophore poroid .... Boletaceae
             (see also Strobilomycetaceae)

9(3). Hymenophoral trama convergent (inverse) .... Pluteaceae
             (Volvariaceae)
9. Hymenophoral trama regular, irregular or subregular 10

10. Spores angular in both lateral and polar view; surface of the spore not ornamented .... Entolomataceae

10. Spores angular in polar view only; surface of the spore warted or spinulose or longitudinally striate 13

11(12). Spores warted or spinulose .... Tricholomataceae

11. Spores longitudinally striate .... Entolomataceae

12. Pileipellis a palisadoderm or epithelium; hymenophoral trama of inflated cells; spores pigmented 13

12. Basidiocarps not with all of the above features 16

13. Spores in mass brownish (rust-colour to hazel brown); ornamented if pinkish brown .... Bolbitiaceae

13. Spores in mass blackish brown (olivaceous black, fuscous black to violaceous black) or if pinkish brown then spores smooth 14

14. Spores not decolorizing or paling in concentrated sulphuric acid 15

14. Spores decolorizing or paling in the above reagent .. Coprinaceae

15. Gills typically mottled; veil not usually evident or if so them pileipellis composed of sphaeropendunculate units .... Coprinaceae

15. Gills not typically mottled; veil usually evident and if overlying a cellular layer then constituent units of the latter not spheropendunculate .... Agaricaceae

16(12). Spores strongly pigmented and never collapsing 17

16. Spores white, cream, ivory or only slightly colored, flushed with lilac, pinkish, yellowish, etc. or if brown in mass then spores thin-walled and often collapsing on drying and hardly coloured s.m .. 21

17. Spores in mass brown 18

17. Spores in mass dark-coloured, umber brown, blackish purple, violaceous, olivaceous or fuscous black 20

18. Spores richly pigmented (ochraceous or rust-colour) 19

18. Spores dull-coloured (snuff brown to hazel brown) .... Cortinariaceae (:Inocybeae)

19. Basidiospores smooth or if ornamented then basidiocarp apparently non-mycorrhizal; velar remains when present sometimes copious but never membranous; chrysocystidia absent .... Cortinariaceae
(:Cortinariaeae)

19. Basidiospores smooth and velar remains often membranous; basidiocarp apparently never mycorrhizal; chrysocystidia absent ....
...... Cortinariaceae
(:Pholiotoideae)

20(17). Gills free or almost so, umber to vandyke brown (ie. red-brown) shades; pileus often fibrillose scaly or roughened; basidia short and squat; chrysocystidia absent .... Agaricaceae

20. Gills typically adnate or modifications of same, violaceous to fuscous or even olivaceous brown; pileus infrequently fibrillose scaly although velar remnants may leave patches; basidia clavate; chrysocystidia often present .... Strophariaceae

21(16). Spores wavy-spiny and globose-ellipsoid in shape ....
...... Thelephoraceae

21. Spores smooth or if ornamented then not of a basic globose-ellipsoid shape with spiny extensions and protrusions 22

22. Basidia 5.5-7 times as long as the length of the spores ....
...... Hygrophoraceae

22. Basidia not conspicuously long, never even up to 5.5 times as long as spores 23

23. Spores cyanophilic, elongate and distinctly ornamented; hymenophoral trama irregular; hymenium wrinkled to venose .. Gomphaceae

23. Not with all of the above features 24

24. Stipe excentric, lateral or absent 25

24. Stipe central 29

25. Gills crisped or split along the edge or notched 26

25. Gills triangular or wedge-shaped in cross section and never crisped or split 27

26. Gills crisped or split along the edge; gloeocystidia absent; basidiospores ellipsoid, non-amyloid .... Schizophyllaceae

26. Gills notched; gloeocystidial hyphae present; basidiospores amyloid, slightly ornamented and subglobose .... Lentinellaceae

27(25). Hymenophoral trama irregular or with some regularity; thick-walled hyphae often intermixed with thinner elements; spores acyanophilic, ellipsoid-oblong to cylindric .... Pleurotaceae

27. Hymenophoral trama regular (or even bilateral) or if irregular then thick-walled hyphae lacking and spores ellipsoid-oblong to cylindric and then cyanophilic 28

28. Spores brownish in mass often collapsing on drying ....
...... Cortinariaceae

28. Spores white, cream or even flushed with lilac or pink to greenish but never more strongly brown than pale buff and not collapsing on drying .... Tricholomataceae

29(24). Hymenophoral trama irregular; basidia 2-8 spored, slender and club-shaped .... Cantharellaceae

29. Hymenophoral trama regular to subregular, or if irregular than basidia not distinctly slender and never more than 4-spored 30

30. Basidiocarps with at least one of the following features:
    a) Spores metachromatic:
    b) Spores amyloid and with smooth to minutely roughened walls;
    c) Spores dextrinoid and with a distinctly to moderately thick, complex, heterogeneous wall .... Lepiotaceae

30. Basidiocarp with none of the above features 31

31. Spores brown in mass and often collapsing on drying ....
...... Cortinariaceae
(:Crepidoteae)

31. Spores white, cream or even flushed with lilac or pink to greenish but never more strongly brown than pale buff and not collapsing on drying .... Tricholomataceae

Agaricaceae

Hymenophoral trama regular to subregular but never intermixed. Basidia often comparatively rather small, usually 4-spored, lacking siderophilous granulation. Basidiospores dark pinkish brown to sepia brown or greenish in mass with thick, stratified, heterogeneous, dextrinoid or inamyloid walls; cyanophilous only when young; smooth to very minutely roughened; a wide range of shapes from ellipsoid to subglobose, inaequilateral, even cross-shaped; generally small to medium, with germ-pore, not truncate, usually a thinning of the outer layers but with a corresponding thickening of inner layers; suprahilar depression or plage absent; hilar apex short, and characteristically often bearing a large circular scar. Cystidia present or absent on margin of gills, not strongly differentiated. Hyphae inamyloid with or without clamp connections, forming a homoiomerous trama. Pileipellis an epithelium, palisadoderm or trichodermial palisade in which the units are almost isodiametric or a cutis of parallel repent hyphae; often masked or modified by presence of velar remains.

1. Pileal surface neither an epithelium nor a cellular 2
1. Pileal surface an epithelium or cellular layer 3

   2. Spores not pseudoamyloid; cheilocystidia absent or if present vesiculose or catenulate . . . . **Agaricus** (459)
   2. Spores distinctly pseudoamyloid; cheilocystidia elongate . . . .
       . . . . . . **Micropsalliota** (467)

3. Spores finely punctate; spore print initially green or olive, becoming purple-brown upon drying . . . . **Melanophyllum** (466)
3. Spores smooth or nodulose, the surface unornamented; spore print not initially green 4

   4. Spores angular or nodulose in outline 5
   4. Spores globose to ovate or subellipsoid, not angular or nodulose in outline . . . . **Agaricus** (459)

5. Pileus shaggy with spinose scales of subisodiametric cells; spores not cross-shaped . . . . **Cystoagaricus** (464)
5. Pileus not shaggy, pileipellis subhymeniform; spores cross-shaped . . .
      . . . . . . **Crucispora** (465)

Note: Agaricaceae is usually associated with **Lepiota** and its allies in a single genus; it is considered more useful to place the pale-spored elements in the separate family Lepiotaceae.

Amanitaceae

Hymenophoral trama bilateral, consisting of often broadened, clavate cells. Basidia not excessively long, 2 or 4-spored, usually the latter; siderophilous granulation lacking. Basidiospores white, cream, greyish or flushed slightly pinkish or greenish in mass, with generally thin, homogeneous, smooth (except in a few species) amyloid or inamyloid, acyanophilic walls; globose to cylindric or bacilliform; usually medium to large; germ-pores and similar modifications absent, although the adaxial surface sometimes shows a distinctive applanation; hilar appendix abrupt, pronounced. Cheilocatenulae present as +/— free, vesiculose cells or chains of cells. Hyphae inamyloid with or without clamp connections, often inflated to form sphaerocytes; forming a homoiomerous trama. Pileipellis a cutis or an ixocutis, often slightly developed because of the presence of a veil.

1. Spores amyloid .... **Amanita** (421)

1. Spores inamyloid 2

    2. Volva present, varying from membranous, well-developed, and saccate, to merely a series of bands or patches on the bulbous base of the stipe (but then the pileal surface with evident remnants of the universal veil) .... **Amanita** (421)

    2. Volva completely absent; no velar remnants on the pileal surface ..
           ...... **Limacella** (430)

Note: **Termitomyces** and **Rhodotus** have formerly been associated with the Amanitaceae but are now better placed in the Tricholomataceae.

Armillariaceae
(See Biannularieae in the Tricholomataceae)

Bolbitiaceae

Hymenophoral trama regular, although usually of inflated lateral units which tend to reduce the mediostratum to a thin, floccose strand of filamentous hyphae. Basidia 1-, 2-, 3-, or 4-spored, often squat, small and broad, thin-walled, lacking siderophilous granulation and frequently accompanied by brachycystidia. Basidiospores rich brown, rust-colour to hazel brown in mass, with thick, pigmented, complex, smooth wall; only rarely slightly ornamented; ovoid-ellipsoid, although some are compressed to appear limoniform (usually large to medium); usually lacking a suprahilar depression; plage absent; hilar-appendix small, although distinct. Cystidia always on the gill-margin, also present on the gill-face in some species; typically thin-walled, rarely thickened except at base. Hyphae with or without clamp connections, inamyloid, frequently highly inflated, forming a homoiomerous trama. Pileipellis a palisadoderm of pyriform to subglobose, pedicellate cells, often with distinct dermatocystidia and pileocystidia, sometimes at margin overlaid by filamentous units from a veil.

1. Pileus viscid; spore print rust brown 2
1. Pileus not viscid or if viscid the spore print fuscous or dark dingy brown 3

    2. Pileus very thin-fleshed and fragile, often collapsing, plicate-sulcate toward the margin .... **Bolbitius** (526)
    2. Pileus at least moderately thick-fleshed, not plicate-sulcate toward the margin .... **Conocybe** (514)

3(1). Spore print bright rust brown; stipe fragile or brittle-cartilaginous, seldom more than 2-3 mm thick .... **Conocybe** (514)
3. Spore print dark milky chocolate to fuscous to dark dingy brown; stipe fleshy-fibrous, 3 mm or more thick .... **Agrocybe** (523)

Note: Several authors split the genus **Conocybe** into four entities; **Conocybe** s. stricto, **Pseudoconocybe**, **Pholiotina** and **Galerella**. Developmental and anatomical characters do not appear to support this splitting. Recently Singer has related **Descolea** to the Bolbitiaceae; in preference this genus is referred to the Cortinariaceae.

Boletaceae

Hymenophoral trama bilateral, often distinctly so, little or no development of hymenopodium. Basidia not excessively long, (3)-4 spored, lacking siderophilous granulation. Basidiospores variable in colour, in mass golden yellow, ferrugineous or with olivaceous hues, with moderately thin to slightly thickened, homogeneous, cyanophilic inamyloid, smooth wall, or strongly ornamented; overall form elongate rounded at apex with sides attenuated apically and basically to give a fusoid outline, boletiform especially in N. hemisphere species, only a few small genera with spores; characteristically ellipsoid to subglobose differences with Strobilomycetaceae should be carefully noted; medium to large often up to 15 um long or even more; germ pore or similar apical modifications infrequent, typically interrupted adaxially by a pronounced suprahilar depression but development variable even with the spores of a single basidiocarp; lacking a suprahilar depression in those spores with longitudinal dimensions less than twice the breadth. Cystidia absent or if present both at mouth of tubes and on tube faces, or only around pores; often elongate, usually thin-walled although in some moderately thickened and in **Tuboseta** thick-walled. Hyphae with or without clamp connections; usually inamyloid forming homoiomerous trama. Pileipellis very variable ranging from a true, distinct cutis to a poorly differentiated cutis, from a trichodermium +/— well-developed to a trichodermial palisade with the units of a chain often swollen to form a pleuristratous layer or the end cells swollen to form an epithelial layer; infrequently obscured by the remains of a veil.

1. Spores always rather short (not more than twice as long as broad; clamp connections constantly present 2
1. Spores elongate (more than twice as long as broad) but if shorter then clamp connections absent (although occasionally present in vegetative mycelium) 6

   2. Spore print yellow; hyphae annularly arranged in cortex of stipe; tubes depressed or subfree around apex of stipe, not arcuate—decurrent .... **Gyroporus**
   2. Spore print some shade of brown, olive-brown to purplish grey-brown; hyphae longitudinally arranged in stipe; tubes adnate to decurrent, more rarely soon depressed around the stipe 3

3. Veil present .... **Paragyrodon**
3. Veil absent 4

4. Basidiocarp large and bulky; tubes soon depressed . . . .
. . . . . . **Phaeogyroporus**

4. Basidiocarp less bulky; stipe eccentric or strongly reduced to absent; tubes more or less arcuate—decurrent 5

5. Spores larger than 5 um; spore print brown with olive tint; stipe usually well developed, central to lateral . . . . **Gyrodon**

5. Spores smaller than 5 um; spore print brown with purplish tint; stipe absent . . . . **Meiorganum**

6(1). Hymenophoral trama (lateral strata) consisting of slightly divergent hyphae, touching each other and not strongly curved outwards, often becoming rather irregular in age and only little paler (if at all) from the mediostratum; tubes angular and wide and often gill-like; veil absent 7

6. Hymenophoral trama (lateral strata) consisting of loosely arranged hyphae curving outwards and generally less pigmented than the mediostratum; tubes sometimes narrow to wide but never gill-like; veil absent or present 8

7. Tubes gill-like . . . . **Phylloporus**
(see Paxillaceae)

7. Tubes distinct . . . . **Xerocomus**

8(6). Clamp connections present in the basidiocarp 9

8. Clamp connections absent in the basidiocarp 10

9. Veil present . . . . **Boletinus**

9. Veil absent . . . . **Psiloboletinus**

10(8). Veil usually present; pileus cortex usually gelatinized; stipe often covered by glandular dots or if these are absent then tubes arranged in radial fashion (boletinoid); spores although elongated, fusoid to cylindric then usually with cinnamon or rust colour in spore print, small and narrow; flesh becoming brightly colored in pinks and lilacs with alkali . . . . **Suillus**

10. Veil usually absent, although when present very distinct; stipe punctate, distinctly to slightly reticulate but never glandular dotted; spores usually elongate but even when ellipsoid (not more than twice as long as broad) broad and spore print less commonly cinnamon or rust-colour; flesh not becoming brightly colored with alkali and if pileus surface changes color with alkali, then only in blues and greens 11

11. Veil present or if absent then stipe viscid .... **Pulveroboletus**

11. Veil absent and stipe rarely viscid, if so then also covered in furfuraceous scales or scabrosities 12

12. Tubes decurrent; stipe at most with powdery granules, never strikingly punctate; tubes cinnamon buff with small pores ....
...... **Chalciporus**

12. Tubes never obviously decurrent; stipe distinctly ornamented at least in some parts, and if punctate then prominently so; spores elongate and broad 13

13. Spore print pink, vinaceous or with similar tints .... **Tylopilus**

13. Spore print ochraceous, olivaceous or some shade of brown 14

14. Spore print yellow-brown or yellow, brightly colored; spores cylindric to rod-shaped, or fusoid-subcylindric and always relatively narrow with a rather thin wall .... **Xanthoconium**

14. Spore print ochraceous, olivaceous or if some shade of yellow then never brightly colored; spores typically subfusoid (boletiform) or broadly ellipsoid (not more than twice as long as broad), never rod-shaped and never with particularly thin wall 15

15. Spore print usually with olivaceous tints; stipe punctate or reticulate, distinctly to only slightly so; tubes usually yellow but occasionally in reds or oranges, frequently bluing and never white or pallid ....
...... **Boletus**

15. Spore print usually with ochraceous or cinnamon tints; stipe floccose, scabrose or woolly punctate, commencing white and remaining so or usually darkening with age to become finally black, brown, etc.; tubes pale colored usually white or pale buff, exceedingly rarely becoming blue although frequently darkening to blackish, brownish, purplish, and always darkening thus if yellow .... **Leccinum**

Cantharellaceae

Hymenophoral trama irregular. Basidia 2-8 spored stichic, slender, club-shaped, lacking siderophilous granulation. Basidiospores white to yellowish, pale ochraceous or salmon in mass, with thin, smooth, inamyloid homogeneous wall, subglobose, ovoid to ellipsoid; lacking suprahilar depression, plage, germ-pore or other modifications; hilar apex quite distinct. Cystidia absent. Hyphae thin-walled, sometimes inflating, with or without clamp connections and becoming secondarily septate to form rows of short unbranched cells.

1. Margin of pileus wavy, incurved at first; clamp connections present; basidiocarp superficially agaricoid 2

1. Margin of pileus entire, straight from beginning or incurved; clamp connections absent; basidiocarp trumpet to funnel-shaped, or irregularly lobed 3

    2. Flesh waxy-firm, not watery .... **Cantharellus**

    2. Flesh watery .... **Goosenia**

3(1). Hyphae copiously secondarily septate to form long chains of moniliform cells; margin incurved at first .... **Pseudocraterellus**

3. Hyphae often short celled, finally thick-walled, more or less inflating; margin straight from beginning .... **Craterellus**

Note: **Pseudocraterellus** is frequently synonimized with **Craterellus** and (except the watery flesh **Goosenia**) appears extremely close to **Cantharellus**. The genus **Clavariadelphus** has frequently been associated with this family.

Coprinaceae

Hymenophoral trama regular or becoming subregular with maturity. Basidia often small or broad with a long pedicel, 2- or 4-spored, in one genus frequently di- or even trimorphic; lacking siderophilous granulation, often accompanied by voluminous brachycystidia. Basidiospores black, fuscous to olivaceous black, sometimes chocolate brown or date brown in mass, dispersed, except in **Panaeolus**, by concentrated sulphuric acid; with thick usually deeply pigmented, complex, smooth, occasionally ornamented walls; wide range of form from subglobose to ovoid, ellipsoid, oblong cylindric, reniform, amygdaliform, citriform, mitriform or hexagonal, not infrequently adaxial-abaxially compressed to appear lenticular; widely varying in size from large to quite small; apex modified usually with an apical or occasionally inclined subapical pore, often giving a truncate appearance, frequently producing a pronounced rim or even short tube; suprahilar depression and plage sometimes present; hilar-apex either poorly or strongly developed. Cystidia frequent on both margin and gill faces occasionally only on margins; thin-walled, less frequently thickened and rarely metuloids; often voluminous and little differentiated. Pileipellis usually a palisadoderm of short, broad cells, sometimes in chains, sometimes pedicellate, and sometimes more ellipsoid and radially arranged; often obscured by the velar remains.

1. Lamellae deliquescing at maturity .... **Coprinus** (489)
1. Lamellae not deliquescing 2

   2. Inaequihymeniiferous (Brachycystidia block-like, almost isodiametric, basidia projecting prominently, regularly spaced, and well separated) .... **Coprinus** (489)
   2. Aequihymeniiferous (Brachycystidia clavate or cylindric, basidia not projecting prominently, or if they do, then they are irregularly spaced) 3

3. Base of the stipe with a conspicuous, ample, saccate, membranous volva. (tropical fungi) .... **Macrometrula** (495)
3. Base of the stipe without a volva 4

   4. Pleurocystidia present in the hymenium 5
   4. Pleurocystidia absent from the hymenium 8

5. Metuloids with thick brownish wall and mucronate apex; context becoming blue or blue-green where bruised .... **Panaeolus** (509)

5. Pleurocystidia either thin-walled or thick-walled, but if the latter, not as in the above; context not staining blue or blue green where bruised 6

6. Pileus viscid .... **Panaeolus** (507)

6. Pileus not viscid 7

7. Pleurocystidia of the chrysocystidial type .... **Panaeolus** (507)

7. Pleurocystidia not of the chrysocystidial type ..... **Psathyrella** (497)

8(4). Spores verrucose, with low warts 9

8. Spores smooth (unornamented) 11

9. Pileus with a superficial layer of colored fibrils, a similar layer also present on the stipe, often forming an annular fibrillose zone ....
...... **Lacrymaria**

9. Pileus and stipe both glabrous, lacking any superficial fibrillose layer 10

10. Spore print black; spores not discolored by treatment with concentrated sulphuric acid; lamellae mottled with the maturing spores .... **Panaeolus** (506)

10. Spore print purple brown; spores discolored to pale slate gray by treatment with concentrated sulphuric acid ..... **Psathyrella** (497)

11(8). Spore print black; spores not discolored by treatment with concentrated sulphuric acid; lamellae mottled with the maturing spores ....
..... **Panaeolus** (507)

11. Spore print purple brown; spores discolored to pale slate gray by treatment with concentrated sulphuric acid; lamellae not mottled with the maturing spores .... **Psathyrella** (497)

Note: **Panaeolus** as here understood includes **Panaeolina**, **Anellaria** and **Copelandia** which really differ very little from **Panaeolus**. Singer includes **Lacrymaria** in **Psathyrella**.

Cortinariaceae

Hymenophoral trama regular to subregular. Basidia clavate not exceptionally long, usually 4-spored, usually lacking siderophilous granulation. Basidiospores some shade of brown in mass, ranging from clay-brown to deep ferruginous, although sometimes umber or even white to pale in exceptional species or genera (eg. **Leucocortinarius**), never with violaceous hue; with stratified, smooth to slightly ornamented to strongly ornamented walls, and outer layer sometimes loosening; cyanophilic in pale spores, or dextrinoid, strongly to weakly pigmented; a wide range of apical modifications found although a germ pore rarely exhibited; with or without suprahilar depression and plage sometimes very distinctly delimited; hilar apex short or quite distinct. Variable in shape, spores often attenuated apically to become mucronate but never truncate, ellipsoid, amygdaliform to nodulose or nodose. Cystidia absent or present usually on the margin of the gills, frequently lacking altogether, more rarely on the gill faces, and even then frequently thick-walled; with or without crystalline deposits. Hyphae thin-walled, inamyloid with or without clamp connections forming a homoiomerous trama. Pileipellis a trichodermium often with differentiated end-cells, a trichodermial palisade, an epithelium or a cutis, uncommonly a palisadoderm of pedicellate cells, sometimes masked by filamentous units from a veil.

KEY TO TRIBES

1. Spore print whitish buff, buff or ochraceous; spores coarsely ornamented with ridges, verrucose, etc. 2

1. Spore print some shade of brown and if buff or ochre then spores smooth or minutely spinulose; pileal surface varies 4

    2. Spore print distinctly dark buff or ochraceous; pileus surface an epithelium or palisade trichodermium of short broad elements . . . .
             . . . . . . Tribe Phaeolepioteae

    2. Spore print pale; pileal surface a cutis or trichodermium but never with swollen units 3

3. Spores with a double or triple wall which strongly reacts with Melzer's reagent (amyloid or dextrinoid); veil absent or only forming a marginal veil and never as a ring; stipe clavate, lacking emarginate bulb .... **Hebelomina**
(Tribe Inocybeae)

3. Spores not with a distinctly double wall, inamyloid; veil often a remnant at margin of emarginate bulb, on stem and at cap margin ....
...... **Leucocortinarius**
(Tribe Cortinarieae)

4(1). Spore wall single-layered, thin, collapsing readily, many spores consequently apearing crumpled (especially when dried material is examined) .... Tribe Tubarieae

4. Spore wall double-layered (at least thick, and not collapsing readily) 5

5. Spores angular-nodulose .... Tribe Inocybeae

5. Spores not angular-nodulose 6

6. Spore wall ornamented 7

6. Spore wall smooth, not ornamented 14

7. Spores with peg-like spines or large rounded nodules ....
...... Tribe Inocybeae

7. Spores punctate-rough to spinulose or verruculose 8

8. Pileus sessile and laterally attached, or at most with a very short lateral or nearly lateral stipe 9

8. Sporocarp stipitate, with central to excentric stipe 11

9. Clamps present 10

9. Clamps absent .... Tribe Crepidoteae

10. Spore print bright rust brown .... Tribe Cortinarieae

10. Spore print yellow-brown to dull brown or umber ....
...... Tribe Crepidoteae

11(8). Spore ornamentation consisting of minute colored spines arising from the inner layer of the spore wall and imbedded in the outer layer —the spore appears punctate, or "stippled" .... Tribe Tubarieae

11. Spore ornamentation exosporial, consisting of punctate, spines, or warts on the outer surface of the spore 12

12. Spore print dull cinnamon brown, yellow brown, fuscous brown, or reddish brown 13

12. Spore print bright rust brown, orange brown, or rich, dark rust brown .... Tribe Cortinarieae

13. Spores spherical, small; pileus white or pale cream color, viscid, with a fringe of hairs on the margin in younger specimens .... Tribe Ripartiteae

13. Not as in the above in all characteristics .... Tribe Inocybeae

14(6). Pileus sessile and laterally or dorsally attached, or at most having a very short lateral stipe or a "pseudostipe" 15

14. Pileus stipitate, the stipe central to excentric 16

15. Spores pale colored in KOH, lacking germ pore .. Tribe Crepidoteae

15. Spores dark coloured in KOH with distinct to indistinct germ pore .. .. Tribe Pholiotoideae

16(14). Spores with a prominent or narrow, indistinct apical germ pore .... Tribe Pholiotoideae

16. Spores lacking an apical germ pore (they may have a callus, however) 17

17. Pileal surface, lower half or two-thirds of the stipe and under surface of the annulus covered with an epithelium; massive, fleshy, terrestrial basidiocarps .... Tribe Phaeolepioteae

17. Epithelium absent, or if one is present, it is confined to the surface of the pileus and the basidiocarps are small and lignicolous......... 18

18. Spore print dull grayish brown, dark rust brown, chocolate brown, fuscous brown, or olivaceous brown 19

18. Spore print bright rust-color, orange brown, or bright yellow brown .... Tribe Cortinarieae

19. Spore print chocolate to fuscous brown or dark rust brown .... Tribe Pholiotoideae

19. Spore print ochraceous to olivaceous brown or dull cinnamon brown to greyish brown .... Tribe Inocybeae

Tribe Cortinarieae

Pleurotoid, centrally to eccentrically stipitate; pileal surface a cutis, trichodermium, ixotrichodermium, epithelium, or viscid pellicle; spores punctate-rough to verruculose, rather infrequently smooth; spore print bright rust brown, orange-tan, or dark, rich rust-color; clamps present or absent.

1. Pileus sessile and laterally or dorsally attached, or with a very short, strongly excentric to lateral stipe (pleurotoid habit), predominantly tropical or subtropical fungi .... **Pyrrhoglossun** (628)

1. Pileus stipitate, the stipe central to somewhat excentric but never lateral 2

   2. Spores whitish buff, cocoanut buff .... **Leucocortinarius** (624)

   2. Spores distinctly colored 3

3. Pileal surface a palisade trichodermium with cystidioid terminal cells; spores smooth with double wall; basidiocarps small, predominently lignicolous .... **Phaeomarasmius** (561)

3. Pileal surface a cutis of repent hyphae, or a viscid pellicle, or an ixotrichodermium; spores punctate-roughened to verruculose, or if smooth, then with a suprahilar plage delimited by a ragged line; size and habitat of the basidiocarp varies 4

   4. Pileal surface viscid 5

   4. Pileal surface not viscid 8

5. Cortina present, at least in young stages .... **Cortinarius** (587)

5. Cortina absent, even in the youngest states 6

   6. Stipe with a long pseudorhiza; spores lacking a suprahilar plage; clamps present .... **Phaeocollybia** (638)

   6. Stipe without a pseudorhiza; spores with a suprahilar plage, or if without one, then clamps are present 7

7. Outer veil squamulose; spores large; cystidia absent ....
      ...... **Cuphocybe** (643)

7. Outer veil not squamulose; spores usually less than 12um or if larger with suprahilar depression and cystidia 8

8(4). Having one or more of the following features:
   a) mycenoid habit;
   b) slender, cartiliaginous stipe;
   c) punctate or warted spores with smooth plage;
   d) punctate or warted spores without a plage and clamps absent in the basidiocarp;
   e) smooth spores .... **Galerina** (629)

8. Not having any of the features listed above 9

9. Basidiocarps lignicolous, brightly colored (yellow, orange, bright rusty tan, rich red-brown, green, etc.); taste often bitter; pileal surface becoming black with 10% KOH .... **Gymnopilus** (625)

9. Basidiocarps terrestrial, varying greatly in color; taste usually not bitter (but may be intensely so in some basidiocarps with viscid pileus); pileal surface may change color with 10% KOH but does not become black 10

10. Partial veil a cortina 11

10. Partial veil membranous, forming a well defined membranous annulus; universal veil forming volvate patches or bands on the stipe base, and giving the pileal disc a white, "glazed" appearance .
...... **Rozites** (586)

11. Anthrachinonic pigments always endocrocin and abundant, small to medium-sized basidiocarps with yellow, orange, green or red lamellae; cylindric to a slightly clavate stipe .... **Dermocybe** (626)

11. Pigments not anthrachinonic, small to large basidiocarps usually lacking distinctly colored gills or if so frequently violaceous or blue ... 12

   12. Spores with distinct plage; pileal surface viscid with blue or violaceous pigments .... **Stephanopus** (623)

   12. Spores lacking plage or if present poorly differentiated and pileus, if violaceous or blue not viscid .... **Cortinarius** (587)

Tribe Crepioteae

Pileus sessile, laterally or dorsally attached, or at most with a very short lateral stipe or pseudostipe; spores smooth to spinulose or punctate; spore print various shades of brown.

1. Basidiocarp with gills, agaricoid 2

1. Basidiocarp without gills, cyphelloid 3

2. Clamp connections absent; spore print cream buff; spores smooth .
...... **Pleurotellus** (658)

2. Clamp connections present or absent; spore print buff, coffee-color, darker than Chamois; spores minutely roughened or if smooth then the basidiocarp with clamp-connections and a distinctly brown spore print .... **Crepidotus** (653)

3(1). Spores punctate .... See **Pellidiscus** and **Chromocyphella** (662)

3. Spores smooth .... See **Phaeosolenia** (661);
...... **Episphaeria** (660); **Merismodes** (663)

Tribe Inocybeae

Pileus centrally to excentrically stipitate; pileal surface a cutis of repent filaments, a trichodermium (often with cystidioid terminal cells), or a viscid pellicle; spores smooth, punctate-roughened, angular-nodulose, verrucose, or with blunt, cylindrical spines, rarely with a discernible germ pore, but sometimes with a callus; spore print dull yellow brown to dull umber or chocolate or fuscous brown; clamps usually present, infrequently lacking.

1. Spores angular-nodulose .... **Inocybe** (569)

1. Spores not angular-nodulose 2

2. Pileal surface viscid 3

2. Pileal surface not viscid 4

3. Spores punctate-roughened to verruculose .... **Hebeloma** (577)

3. Spores smooth .... **Inocybe** (569)

4(2). Spores ornamented (punctate-roughened to verrucose or spiny) .
...... 5

4. Spores smooth, unornamented 7

5. Spores whitish buff, creamish buff .... **Hebelomina** (580)

5. Spores distinctly colored 6

6. Spores punctate-roughened; pileal surface a layer of pileocystidia, or a palisade trichodermium with cystidioid terminal cells; basidiocarps associated with **Alnus** or occasionally with **Salix** ... **Naucoria**
...... (=**Alnicola**) (582)

6. Spores coarsely verrucose, or covered with blunt, cylindrical spine; pileal surface without pileocystidia and not a palisade trichodermium with cystidioid terminal cells; basidiocarps not associated (regularly, at any rate) with **Alnus** or **Salix** ... **Inocybe** (569)

7(5). Pileal surface with abundant pileocystidia composing a loose trichodermium; basidiocarps small, often with a slender, cartilaginous stipe
...... **Simocybe** (651)

7. Pileal surface without pileocystidia or at most with infrequent and scattered ones in a trichodermium; often marked with velar remnants; size of basidiocarp and thickness of stipe varying ....
...... **Inocybe** (569)

Tribe Phaeolepioteae

Centrally stipitate; pileal surface an epithelium or palisade trichodermium with short, inflated cells; annulus present, well developed; spores smooth or punctate-roughened; spore print buff, brownish ochraceous, or ochraceous tawny.

1. Epithelium present on lower part of stipe and under surface of the annulus; spores smooth; basidiocarps associated with boreal conifers and hardwoods .... **Phaeolepiota** (481)

1. No epithelium on the stipe or annulus; spores punctate-rough; basidiocarps associated with **Nothofagus** (Southern Hemisphere) etc. ....
...... **Descolea** (520)

Tribe Pholiotoideae

Basidiocarp centrally or laterally stipitate; pileal surface a cutis; annulus present or absent, often well developed; spores smooth or only very faintly ornamented; spore print rich red-brown.

1. Basidiocarp excentric to laterally stipitate .... **Pleuroflammula** (560)

1. Basidiocarp centrally stipitate 2

2. Basidiocarp with pleurocystidia, often in the form of chrysocystidia
..... **Pholiota** (540)

2. Basidiocarp lacking pleurocystidia 3

3. Basidiocarp strongly hygrophanous; spores dull brown in KOH ....
...... **Kuehneromyces** (555)

3. Basidiocarp weakly hygrophanous or if slightly hygrophanous then
the pileal surface squamulose; spores bright brown in KOH ....
.... **Pachylepyrium** (558)

Tribe Ripartiteae

Basidiocarp centrally stipitate, lamellae subdecurrent; pileal surface
viscid, with a fringe of marginal hairs, spores small, isodiametric, finely
punctate-roughened; spore print grayish clay color.

One genus .... **Ripartites** (692)

Tribe Tubarieae

Centrally stipitate basidiocarps, rarely excentrically stipitate.
Lamellae adnate or subdecurrent; pileal surface of repent or tangled
filamentous hyphae or with elements bunched together to form a
trichodermium with end-cells more or less broadened or an epithelium;
spores with a single-layered wall, smooth readily collapsing or with two
thin layers, the inner layer bearing spines that are imbedded in the outer
layer, hence the spore appearing punctate; spore print ochre brown to
ferrugineous or flushed olivaceous, clamp connections usually present.

1. Spores smooth 2

1. Spores ornamented 3

2. Pileal surface a cutis .... **Tubaria** (647)

2. Pileal surface an epithelum .... **Flammulaster** (561)

3. Pileal surface a cutis; lamellae adnate to decurrent; spores smooth or
minutely ornamented with homogeneous wall .... **Tubaria** (647)

3. Pileal surface a trichodermium often poorly differentiated or if a cutis
the the spore wall heterogeneous and ornamented ....
...... **Melanomphalia** (649)

Entolomataceae

Hymenophoral trama regular in the lateral strata often appearing irregular and denser in an outer layer (hymenopodium); subhymenium often of strikingly shortened elements. Basidia not excessively long, 4-spored, although sometimes consistently 2-spored, with some siderophilous granulation. Basidiospores greyish pink to pinkish cinnamon in mass, with thin, often collapsing, 2-layered, smooth, inamyloid cyanophilic walls; characteristically in all optical or at least in polar view, nodose to nodulose or angular; apart from angularity spores vary overall in shape from globose, ellipsoid to fusiform; germ-pore and similar modifications absent; suprahilar depression usually present and hilar appendix prominent. Cystidia absent or present on the margin or on both margin and face, generally not highly differentiated. Hyphae inamyloid, with or without clamp connections, sometimes modified into lactifers, forming a homoiomerous trama. Pileipellis varying from a well formed to ill defined cutis of filamentous units, to a well defined to irregular trichodermial palisade, rarely a true trichodermium, infrequently gelatinized although filamentous units may become agglutinated to form scales.

1. Spores angular in polar view only 2

1. Spores angular in all views 3

  2. Spores longitudinally striate in lateral view ...... **Clitopilus** (667)

  2. Spores rough to warty in lateral view .... **Rhodocybe** (669)

3(2). Stipe excentric, lateral or missing, basidiocarps never tricholomatoid .... **Claudopus**

3. Stipe present central 4

  4. Pileus minutely tomentulose (at least on the disc), squamulose, or distinctly appressed-fibrillose; usually collybioid to mycenoid to omphalinoid 5

  4. Pileus glabrous, hoary, or covered with a layer of minute fibrils and then appearing micaceous-like; viscid, dry or lubricous; tricholmatoid, collybioid, or mycenoid 7

5. Stipe base strigose; tramal hyphae of the pileus with incrusted, distinctly thickened (0.2-0.5um or more) brownish walls ..... **Pouzarella**

5. Stipe base naked or covered by a cottony mycelium; tramal hyphae, if incrusted, thin walled 6

6. Pileipellis an irregular to entangled layer of hyphae; young basidiocarps usually entirely white to cinereous .... **Alboleptonia**

6. Pileipellis usually a trichodermium or nearly hymeniform at least on the disc; if an entangled layer of hyphae then the basidiocarps some color other than white .... **Leptonia**

7(4). Basidiocarps unquestionably mycenoid or collybioid ..... **Nolanea**

7. Basidiocarps not as above 8

8. Basidiocarps unquestionably tricholomatoid, always with a fleshy-fibrous stipe .... **Entoloma**

8. Basidocarps not as above 9

9. Pigment incrusted on the walls of some hyphae of the pileipellis .....
...... **Nolanea**

9. Pigment in the vacuoles of the hyphae of the pileipellis 10

10. Clamp connections scattered to abundant on the hyphae of the pileipellis; urea concentration low, 0 to +1 .... **Entoloma**

10. Clamp connections absent or rare on the hyphae of the pileipellis; urea concentration high, +4 to +5 .... **Nolanea**

Note: Some agaricologists (Kühner & Romagnesi, Singer) place all of the agarics with pink spores, angular in all views, into the genus **Rhodophyllus**; others place these agarics into the genus **Entoloma**. Still others (eg P.D. Orton) recognize the Friesian genera, **Entoloma Nolanea**, **Eccilia**, **Claudopus**, and **Leptonia**, more or less in the sense of Fries. The key presented above was published by one of us (D.L.) in 1974 (Mycologia 66: 991-992).

For those individuals who recognize the genus **Rhodophyllus**, the above genera are presented as subgenera in the family Rhodophyllaceae.

Gomphaceae

Hymenophoral trama irregular. Basidia often quite slender, club-shaped, 2-4-spored, chiastic. Basidiospores ochraceous brown, or straw-colored, cream or practically colorless in mass, with moderately thick, roughened (with minute granules, warts, spines, ridges) rarely almost smooth, inamyloid, cyanophilic walls; ellipsoid or more elongated amygdaliform to subcylindrical; usually large; hilar apex fairly prominent. Cystidia rare and then apparently hymenial leptocystidia gloeocysdidia although present, exceptional. Hyphae thin-walled often inflating, becoming slightly thick-walled, usually with clamp connections and often sieve-like structures at some septa, forming a homoiomerous trama. Pileipellis a tangled layer of filamentous units overlaid by more or less undifferentiated, erect or repent inflated, often disarticulating hyphae, often secondarily septate.

1. Gloeocystidia present .... **Gloeocantharellus** (792)

1. Gloeocystidia absent .... **Gomphus**

Gomphidiaceae

Hymenophoral trama bilateral from a central evanescent mediostratum and forming a broad, strongly interwoven hymenopodium; not clearly differentiated from subhymenium. Basidia rather long when mature although never 5.5-7 times as long as the spores, 4-spored, lacking siderophilous granules. Basidiospores smoke grey to fuliginous, purplish or olivaceous black in mass, with moderately thin, cyanophilic, smooth, generally inamyloid walls; characteristically elongate (boletiform) and typically large (between 15 and 30um long), germ-pore and similar modifications absent but with a well-developed suprahilar depression. Cystidia usually oleocystidia on margin and face of gills; distinctly incrusted by a resionous, chestnut to fulvous colored, amorphous material; thin or thick walled. Hyphae amyloid (**Chroogomphus**) to weakly pseudoamyloid or inamyloid (**Gomphidius**), without clamp connections in the basidiocarp except in tomentum of stipe-base, and forming a homoiomerous trama. Pileipellis a trichodermium, often ill-defined and either obliterated by highly gelatinized velar remnants or by compaction from filamentous, gelatinized (or not) hyphae or by swollen cells in **Cystogomphus**.

1. Pileal or lamellar context, or both, amyloid ..... **Chroogomphus** (698)

1. Pileal and lamellar trama inamyloid, or less frequently, dextrinoid . 2

   2. Velar tissue consisting of sphaerocytes ...... **Cystogomphus** (695)

   2. Velar tissue a gelatinous pellicle .... **Gomphidius** (695)

Hygrophoraceae

Hymenophoral trama, irregular to intermixed, or regular, or bilateral (usually in veiled forms). Basidia 5.5-7 times as long as length of spore, 2 or 4-spored, siderophilous granulation lacking; sterigmata often long and prominent. Basidiospores white or whitish in mass, with thin, homogeneous, smooth (except in one genue) inamyloid walls (except in one genus), often containing large refractive oil-guttules, and/or minute guttules which can lie close to the endosporium giving a punctate appearance to the wall; globose to ovoid-ellipsoid in general but varying up to cylindric; varying in size and shape even within spores of a single basidiocarp; germ-pores and similar modifications absent; hilar appendix relatively short. Cystidia absent or rather inconspicuous, or replaced by hyphal like extensions of hymenial constituents; basidioles filamentous. Hyphae inamyloid usually with numerous clamp connections, although absent in two genera; forming a homoiomerous trama. Pileipellis often of a dense radially arranged, layer of filamentous hyphae or varying from a poorly differentiated trichodermial palisade, superficially resembling a hymeniderm, to a layer of repent to erect hyphae, sometimes gelatinized.

1. All parts of the basidiocarp exuding a latex when cut (Tropical Asiatic, African fungi) .... **Bertrandia** (207)

1. Not exuding a latex where cut 2

  2. Hymenophoral trama divergent; often with velar remains ....
       ...... **Hygrophorus** (197)

  2. Hymenophoral trama regular to irregular; lacking velar remains ..
       ...... **Hygrocybe** (200, 202, 204, 206, 207)

Note: **Hygrocybe** as here understood contains a whole range of segregate genera of the old Friesian genus, **Hygrophorus**. **Bertrandia** is taken by Singer as an extension of **Hygrocybe**.

Lentinellaceae

Hymenophoral trama irregular. Basidia 4-spored, clavate. Basidiospores white or pale cream in mass, with thin, minutely echinulate to minutely verrucose, amyloid wall, subglobose to ellipsoid and minute to small; lacking suprahilar depression and plage; germ-pore and apical modifications absent; hilar apex small. Cystidia gloeocystidia with oily contents prominent and staining or darkening in sulpho-aldehyde solutions and staining blue in cotton-blue. Hyphae thin-walled with clamp connections and intermixed with some thick-walled units and a gloeosystem.

One genus .... **Lentinellus** (794)

Auriscalpium is often placed with **Lentinellus** in the Auriscalpiaceae; we prefer to emphasize the differences between the lamellar and hydnoid hymenophore configuration. Additionally, Singer does not discuss the Lentinellaceae in his book.

Lepiotaceae

Hymenphoral trama regular to subregular but never intermixed. Basidia occasionally comparatively small, usually 4-spored, lacking siderophilous granulation. Basidiospores pinkish cream to white or greenish in mass, with distinctly thick to moderately thick, complex, heterogeneous, dextrinoid, amyloid or inamyloid, smooth to very minutely roughened wall; metachromatic with cresyl blue or not; cyanophilic, exhibiting a wide range of apical modifications ranging from discontinuous to a thickened episporium; broad to indistinct germ-pore or lacking germ pore; a wide range of shapes from ellipsoid to subglobose, projectile-shaped, fusoid (etc.); small to large; suprahilar depression and plage absent; hilar-apex short. Cystidia present or absent on margin of gills not strongly differentiated. Hyphae inamyloid or sometimes amyloid with or without clamp connections forming a homoiomerous trama. Pileipellis an epithelium or palisadoderm or a trichodermial palisade with isodiametric units, or a cutis of parallel repent hyphae often marked or modified by presence of velar remains, or a mixture of filamentous hyphae and sphaerocytes.

1. Spores amyloid .... **Lepiota** (472)
1. Spores inamyloid or dextrinoid 2

  2. Spores inamyloid (and not dextrinoid) 3
  2. Spores dextrinoid 7

3. Pileal surface hymeniform 4
3. Pileal surface not hymeniform 5

  4. Spore print ochraceous cream color .... **Chamaemyces** (469)
  4. Spore print white .... **Lepiota** (472)

5(3). Pileal surface an epithelium (tropical fungi) .... **Cystolepiota** (471)

5. Pileal surface a filamentous cutis, with or without intermixed sphaerocytes 6

    6. Veil present in the form of velar patches or an indistinct volva, and
with a well developed ring .... **Smithiomyces** (470)

    6. Veil present only as verrucose scales; surface without sphaerocytes
...... **Hiatulopsis** (475)

7(2). Well developed, cup-shaped volva present 8

7. Volva absent (but the base of the stipe may have conspicuous, more or
less marginate bulb) 9

    8. Spore print green to olive green; spores less than 10um long (fungi
of Asiatic tropics) .... **Clarkeinda** (445)

    8. Spore print white; spores more than 10um long (fungi of South
America) .... **Volvolepiota** (448)

9(7). Spore print green or olive-green .... **Chlorophyllum** (447)

9. Spore print white, cream color, buff or pink 10

    10. Spore print buff; spores entirely blue in cresyl blue (i.e., not meta-
chromatic), with a broad apical germ pore; clamps absent in the
tissue of the annulus .... **Chlorophyllum** (447)

    10. Not with the above combination of characteristics 11

11. Spores not metachromatic in cresyl blue, and without apical germ
pore 12

11. Spores distinctly metachromatic in cresyl blue and with an apical
germ pore 13

    12. Pileal surface entirely of repent filamentous hyphae, veil absent
or very fugacious .... **Pseudobaeospora** (485)

    12. Pileal surface a trichodermium or an interrupted cutis; veil dis-
tinct on pileus and/or stipe .... **Lepiota** (472)

13(11). Spores ornamented .... **Leucoagaricus** (449)

13. Spores smooth 14

The family joins together two distinct tribes of the Agaricaceae in the sense of Singer, united on their poorly pigmented spores. **Cystoderm´**and its allies also placed in the Agaricaceae by some authors are to be included in the Tricholomataceae.

Paxillaceae

Hymenophoral trama more or less bilateral with divergent lateral stratum, or with regular mediostratum and regular to irregular lateral stratum which is divergent towards the subhymenium. Basidia not excessively long, elongate clavate to clavate, 4-spored, lacking siderophilous granulation. Basidiospores dark buff, coffee brown to olivaceous brown in mass, with fairly thin although complex, smooth (except in **Neopaxillus**) wall; dextrinoid or inamyloid; cyanophilic; subglobose to ovoid, ellipsoid to ellipsoid oblong or fusoid; lacking germ-pore and usually any evidence of apical modification; with or without supra-hilar depression; hilar appendix short although distinct. Hyphae inamyloid, with or without clamp connections, forming a homoiomerous trama. Pileipellis a trichodermium, often ill-defined, consisting of erect or repent filamentous hyphae with +/− differentiated end-cells; only partly modified by velar material in one section of **Paxillus**.

2. Gills brightly colored, waxy often anastomosing or becoming sub-poriform, fairly thick with distinct pleuro-and cheilocystidia; spores usually subfusiform .... **Phylloporus**

2. Gills ochraceous, brownish yellow, not particularly thick; spores ellipsoid, cystidia less distinct .... **Paxillus**

Linderomyces has been classified in the Paxillaceae in the past but it has been conclusively shown this is synonymous with **Gloeocantharellus** (Gomphaceae). **Phylloporus** is frequently included in the Boletaceae but on the basis of Australian and S.E. Asian species of this genus it is better placed in the Paxillaceae.

Pleurotaceae

Hymenophoral trama irregular or with some regularity, often with thick-walled hyphae intermixed with thinner elements. Basidia neither extremely long nor extremely narrow, clavate, mostly 4-spored. Basidiospores white to cream or flushed pink to lilac in mass, with thin, smooth, inamyloid and cyanophilous walls; ellipsoid-oblong to cylindric; lacking germ pore, plage and suprahilar depression; hilar appendix generally poorly developed. Cystidia present or absent, not highly differentiated in shape, usually on gill margin, and sometimes thick-walled. Hyphae ranging from generative, skeletal to ligative, never intermixed with laticiferous but oleiferous hyphae sometimes present; inamyloid except in cortex of stipe base; usually with clamp connections in non-differentiated hyphae. Pileipellis varying from a cutis to a trichoderm, or trichodermial palisade often poorly differentiated.

1. Hymenophore consisting of radial veins, rarely as very narrow lamel-lae; pseudoamyloid metuloids and endocystidia present ....
...... **Geopetalum** (193)

1. Distinct lamellae present, metuloids rare and if present never pseudo-amyloid 2

2. Spore print distinctly pink when fresh; spores small, allantoid; pileus covered with a hygrophanous tomentum ....
...... **Phyllotopsis** (180)

2. Spore print white to cream or even pale lilac, if pink then pileus glabrous 3

3. Hyphal system monomitic with thin or thickened walls; spore print varies; cheilocystidia forming a sterile gill edge; pleurocystidia present or absent but never metuloid .... **Pleurotus** (181)

3. Hyphal system di- or trimitic with either skeletal or ligative hyphae; spore print white or at most cream; cystidiform, thin-walled hairs arising directly from the trama and forming a sterile gill edge; pleurocystidia absent or if present then metuloid .... **Lentinus** (189)

Panus often cited as a distinct genus is herein included under **Lentinus**. Singer places these genera into the tribe Lentineae of the family Polyporaceae. One of us (R.W.) prefers to place these in their own family, the Pleurotaceae, thereby, stressing the lamellate nature of the hymenophore.

Pluteaceae

Hymenophoral trama inverse in mature basidiocarps. Basidia not excessively long, 2- or 4-spored, siderophilous granulation lacking. Basidiospores sordid pink to brownish pink in mass, with generally thin, or moderately thick, homogeneous, smooth, non-amyloid, cyanophilic walls; ovoid, globose obovoid to elongate ellipsoid; in most cases not exceeding 10um (although important exceptions); germ pores and similar modifications absent; usually lacking suprahilar depression or applanation; hilar appendix short. Cystidia usually present, often very conspicuous, marginal and/or facial, thin or thick walled. Hyphae inamyloid with or without clamp connections forming a homoiomerous trama. Pileipellis a palisadoderm of sphaeropedunculate cells, or of filamentous hyphae with allantoid or cylindric fusoid end cells.

1. Volva present (annulus absent) .... **Volvariella** (432)

1. Volva absent 2

2. Annulus present .... **Chamaeota** (434)

2. Annulus absent .... **Pluteus** (435)

Note: Several Agaricologists place these genera into the Volvariaceae, although the correct name is Pluteaceae.

Russulaceae

Hymenophoral trama subregular to irregular, or intermixed usually with nests of or individual sphaerocysts. Basidia not excessively long, 2- or 4-spored, lacking siderophilous granulation. Basidiospores white to pale orange in mass, even with a pinkish tinge, with thick, complex, variously ornamented wall with amyloid verrucae, spines or crests underlaid by a further cyanophilic ornamentation; globose ovoid to ellipsoid or occasionally oblong and exceeding 12um in length or diameter; germ pore and similar modifications absent although an amyloid or inamyloid suprahilar plage is usually present; hilar-appendix often very large and conspicuous. cystidia usually present on margin and face of gills as macrocystidia, pseudocystidia or gloeocystidia, or only at margin as cystidiole-like cells. Hyphae inamyloid forming a trama of inflated cells (sphaerocysts) dispersed amongst filamentous units (connective hyphae), forming a heteromerous trama; without clamp connections except in a few species and then only in the stipe trama; often with gloeovessels, latciciferous or oleiferous hyphae. Pileipellis varying in structure from a dense layer or at most consisting of up to three distinct layers, frequently intermixed with macrocystidia to form a turf, or even forming a palisadoderm with rounded cells, or ciliate dermatocystidia which may finally collapse; infrequently covered in velar remains.

1. Latex present, exuding when the basidiocarp is cut; lamellar trama usually without sphaerocysts (except near the base) . **Lactarius** (779)

1. Latex absent; lamellar trama usually with sphaerocysts . . . .
. . . . . . **Russula** (757)

Schizophyllaceae

Hymenophoral trama irregular. Basidia club-shaped, chiastic, 2-4-spored. Basidiospores white, off-white to pinkish in mass, with very thin, smooth, inamyloid, homogeneous wall; narrowly cylindric to slightly allantoid to broadly ellipsoid or cylindric, sometimes associated with a mucilaginous sheath; lacking suprahilar depression or apical modifications; hilar appendix, smooth. Cystidia absent replaced by proliferating hyphae. Hyphae thin to thick walled, not inflating, with clamp connections and frequently with small papillate processes. Pileipellis an interwoven layer of thin to thick walled hyphae forming a mat.

Only one genus . . . . **Schizophyllum** (801)

Strobilomycetaceae

Similar in all respects to Boletaceae. Hymenophoral trama bilateral. Basidia often voluminous, 4-spored, lacking siderophilous granulation. Basidiospores dark-coloured, brown to black in mass, with strongly ornamented rarely smooth, deeply pigmented, complex walls; globose or subglobose to boletiform usually large often extremely so (20-30um), suprahilar plage often present and hilar appendix often conspicuous. Cystidia voluminous both on gill margin and face, thin or moderately, thick walled, often filled with dark material at maturity or after drying. Pileipellis often obscured by units of metavelangiocarpic development but varying from a trichodermium to a trichodermial palisade.

1. Spores globose to ellipsoid, strongly ornamented; spore print blackish brown; tubes white to grey at first, becoming darker with age; veil present . . . . **Strobilomyces** (744)

1. Spores fusoid, cylindric, subfusiform; spore print olivaceous brown to olivaceous black to reddish brown 2

    2. Basidiocarp with gills . . . . **Phylloboletellus** (752)

    2. Basidiocarp with tubes 3

3. Tubes and pores initially white to pale greyish or dull cream becoming light purplish vinaceous or otherwise darker with age; spore print reddish brown . . . . **Porphyrellus** (745)

3. Tubes yellow initially becoming honey-color or olivaceous to olive black, not reddish brown when fresh . . . . **Boletellus** (749)

Strophariaceae

Hymenophoral trama regular. Basidia not excessively long, 2- or 4-spored, lacking siderophilous granulation. Basidiospores dark brown to fuscous or violaceous black in mass, with thick, deeply pigmented, complex, smooth wall only rarely slightly ornamented; ovoid to ellipsoid with adaxial applanation or compressed to appear lentiform or cordiform; large to small; apex usually modified, protracted with a reduced episporial layer, or more frequently truncated by a broad germ pore; suprahilar depression present or absent, but plage absent, hilar appendix fairly prominent. Cystidia well differentiated on gill margin, frequently on gill face also, and there usually accompanied or replaced by chrysocystidia which are characteristically clavate or clavate mucronate. Hyphae usually with clamp connections, inamyloid, forming a homoiomerous trama. Pileipellis a cutis of repent filamentous hyphae the desposition of which may be frequently masked by overlying filamentous velar remains, or hyphae erect to suberect to form a trichodermium which in some species approaching an epithelium in structure constituents often strongly coloured and/or incrusted, and frequently overlying subcellular units.

1. Stipe excentric to lateral or occasionally rudimentary, when present shorter than the diameter of the pileus, and strongly curved (predominantly tropical species) .... **Melanotus** (543)
1. Stipe central to somewhat excentric, not short and curved as in the above 2

  2. Chrysocystidia present in the hymenium 3
  2. Chrysocystidia absent from the hymenium 4

3. Pileal surface with a subcellular hypoderm .... **Hypholoma** (533)
3. Pileal surface lacking a subcellular hypoderm ...... **Stropharia** (530)

  4(2). Spore print cinnamon brown to umber or olivaceous umber; spores in KOH dark honey color under the microscope, without olive or fuscous cast, and without a reddish chestnut line seen inside the endosporium at a point just above optical section ....
      ...... **Kuehneromyces** (557)
  4. Spore print deep lilac or purple, or blackish purple or dark sepia or fuscous; spores in KOH olive brown tinged with fuscous as seen under the microscope, usually with a reddish chestnut line inside the endosporium seen at a point just above optical section 5

5. Basidiocarp (especially the base of the stipe) staining blue or greenish blue where handled .... **Psilocybe** (536)
5. Basidiocarp not staining blue or greenish blue where handled 6

  6. Stipe viscid (from a viscid universal veil) .... **Stropharia** (530)
  6. Stipe not viscid (the pileus may be viscid, however ....
      ...... **Psilocybe** (536)

This family usually also includes **Pholiota** and its allies which we prefer to associate within the Cortinariaceae. **Hypholoma** is used here instead of **Naematoloma** which is frequently found in texts.

Thelephoraceae

Hymenophoral trama sub-regular. Basidia club-shaped, 4-spored (should be chiastic). Basidiospores whitish in mass, globose to ellipsoid—pentangular in form, but wall producing irregular spines which give it a sinuose-irregular outline; inamyloid-subdextrinoid, non-metachromatic in cotton blue; without germ pore and suprahilar depression. Cystidia apparently absent. Hyphae thin-walled with clamp connections, perhaps thickening with maturity forming a homoiomerous trama. Pileipellis of inflated cells in a hymeniderm.

1. Sporocarp with distinct gills .... **Horakia** (484)
1. Sporocarp often multipileate with wrinkles and folds ....
...... **Polyozellus** (798)

> **Horakia** is the correct name for **Verrucospora**. These two genera here are related to **Tomentella**, **Thelephora**, **Boletopsis** and **Scytinopogon** in virtue of their spore characters and hyphal construction.

Tricholomataceae

Hymenophoral trama intermixed, irregular, subregular to regular, less commonly bilateral. Basidia 1-4-spored, clavate, not excessively long, in one group with siderophilous granulation and in some species becoming thick walled. Basidiospores never dark coloured in mass, although varying from pure white to buff, cream, ochre, pinkish or pale hilaceous, with thin to moderately thick, less frequently very thick walled; often collapsing; smooth or strongly ornamented usually the former; homogeneous or heterogeneous, inamyloid or amyloid, rarely dextrinoid generally acyanophilous; lacking a germ pore but an ornamented or smooth suprahilar plage may be present, extremely variable in shape, from small to large, globose to subglobose, to ellipsoid, fusoid, lacrymoid, tonodulose or goniosporic, etc. Cystidia present or absent, or replaced by pseudocystidia on gill margin and/or face usually restricted to the former, often highly diferentiated. Hyphae with thick or thin walls, partly gelatinized or not, inamyloid, amyloid or dextronoid, with or without clamp connection forming homoiomerous trama. Pileipellis varying from a palisadoderm to a trichodermial palisade often with well differentiated end cells, to a trichoderm, or a cutis of filamentous units in some species marked by presence of velar remnants.

> The Tricholomataceae apparently is a heterogeneous group of agarics brought together more on a set of negative characters than any one positive uniting factor. Undoubtedly many of the genera included in the Tricholomataceae are related to each other but how closely or distantly it is rather difficult to ascertain; equally some genera because of our limited

knowledge have been placed in this family for want of a better placement, e.g. **Macrocystidia**, and undoubtedly there is little doubt **Hygrocybe** as outlined by some authors is more closely related to the Tricholomataceae, despite the elongate basidia than to others in the Hygrophoraceae. The distinction between the subfamilies Collybieae and Marasmieae is very tenuous but if they were fused it would make the latter grouping more difficult to define.

Many of the tricholomatoid genera are closely related to some of the cyphelloid groups and these have been included in the key below. Cyphellaceous members are found in four of the eleven subfamilies but it is difficult to separate those referable to the Collybieae and Marasmieae, again suggesting a great affinity between the two. Cyphellaceuos fungi are only found in one other group, i.e. that including **Crepidotus**.

The following key to subfamilies is offered to place the common and widespread members of this complex family. Although the divisions should apply to all possible members of this group from all corners of the world, there may be some discrepancies in the very poorly known species.

KEY TO TRIBES

1. Gills distinctly formed or hymenophore distinctly venose or even tubulose 2
1. Gills absent, veins or gills only exceptionally formed, hymenophore smooth 22

  2. Basidia with siderophilous granulation; basidiocarp usually whitish or dull colored in greys and brown, but if yellow, violaceous or pinkish the pigment not incrusting .... Lyophylleae

  2. Basidia without siderophilous granulation; basidiocarps generally more distinctly colored, with pigments vacuolar, intracellular or incrusting 3

3. Basidiospores amyloid 4
3. Basidiospores inamyloid 8

  4. Hymenophoral trama distinctly bilateral and basidiocarp with distinct velar remnants .... Biannularieae
  4. Hymenophoral trama regular to subregular, if bilateral then only slightly so and rarely into maturity and then never with velar remnants 5

5. Basidiocarp tough, pleurotoid with some gelatinization in the filamentous hymenophoral trama; hymenophore lamellate or tubulose ......
      ...... Panelleae
5. Basidiocarp fleshy, rarely if ever pleurotoid, lacking gelatinized zones or if these are present hyphae inflated and pseudoamyloid 6

6. Basidiocarp usually small, fleshy, +/− cartilaginous; stipe hyphae of basidiocarp often pseudoamyloid; hymenophoral trama of inflated, voluminous, usually pseudoamyloid elements .... Myceneae

6. Basidiocarp not with the above combination of features 7

7. Pileipellis an epithelium, a trichodermial palisade or hymeniform ....
...... Cystodermateae

7. Pileipellis a cutis .... Leucopaxilleae

8(3). Basidiospores distinctly pigmented in mass (pinks and pale cinnamons) and asperulate; basidiocarp pleurotoid to pluteoid; hymenophoral trama distinctly bilateral .... Rhodoteae

8. Not with the above combination of features 9

9. Basidiocarps with at least one of the following features:
   a) pileipellis an epithelium, a trichodermial palisade or hymeniform
   b) pileipellis with broom cells;
   c) stipitipellis an epithelium; 10

9. Basidiocarps not as above 15

10. Hymenophoral trama bilateral, often only slightly but never the less distinctly so; metuloids absent and basidiocarps not reviving after drying .... Pseudohiatuleae

10. Hymenophoral trama regular in mature basidiocarps; metuloids and broom cells can be present 11

11. Metuloids often present; basidiocarp with some gelatinized zones, pleurotoid; hymenophore lamellate .... Resupinateae

11. Metuloids infrequent; basidiocarp lacking gelatinized zones, rarely pleurotoid or if slightly so then never gelatinized; often with dark setiform stipe; hymenophore lamellate to lamellose anastomosing, poroid or merulioid 12

12. Pileipellis or stipitipellis with sphaerocytes ..... Cystodermateae

12. Pileipellis or stipitipellis without sphaerocytes 13

13. Pileipellis with broom cells .... Marasmieae

13. Pileipellis without broom cells 14

14. Hyphae of the trama of the stipe or the pilo- or pileocystidia pseudoamyloid .... Marasmieae

14. Hyphae of the trama of the stipe and the pilo- or pileocystidia inamyloid .... Cystodermateae

15(9). Pileipellis a cutis composed at least in part of diverticulate units or accompanied by diverticulate sphaerocytes . . . . Myceneae

15. Pileipellis a cutis or cellular to a trichodermium and lacking diverticulate units 16

16. Hymenophoral trama bilateral . . . . Pseudohiatuleae

16. Hymenophoral trama regular (in mature basidiocarps) 17

17. Basidiospores ornamented . . . . Clitocybeae

17. Basidiospores smooth 18

18. Pileipellis a trichodermium or a rameales structure 19

18. Pileipellis a cutis or a dense structure 20

19. Basidiocarps with one of the following features:
   a) pileipellis a rameales structure;
   b) pleurotoid habit and with clamp connections;
   c) habit variable but not pleurotoid and without clamp connections . . . . . . Collybieae

19. Basidiocarps not as above; habit tricholomatoid and with clamped hyphae . . . . Cystodermateae

20(18). Clamp connections present . . . . Clitocybeae

20. Clamp connections absent 21

21. Having at least one of the following features:
   a) spores with a necropigment;
   b) habitat decidely tricholomatoid, clitocyboid, or omphalinoid;
   c) basidiocarp with black rhizomorphs;
   d) basidiocarp associated with termite nests;
   e) gloeocystidia present;
   f) habit pleurotoid but with decurrent gills . . . . Clitocybeae

21. Basidiocarps not as above, most often Collybioid, if Pleurotoid, the gills are not decurrent . . . . Collybieae

22. Basidiocarp a stipitate hollow head with pseudocystidia and/or covered with long surface hairs . . . . Marasmieae

22. Basidiocarp lacking long surface hairs and never a stipitate hollow head 23

23. Entirely or some region of the basidiocarp gelatinized or if poorly gelatinized then surface not highly differentiated ...... Resupinateae

23. Basidiocarp not gelatinized or if showing some gelatinization with age then surface with capitate or subcapitate dermatocystidia or with a trichodermium (+/— with broom cells) 24

24. Surface a trichodermium +/— with broom cells; basidiocarp lacking inflated and voluminous units .... Collybieae

24. Surface with capitate or subcapitate dermatocystidia; basidiocarp at least with some inflated and voluminous units .... Myceneae

Tribe Biannularieae

1. Annulus double (two annuli, one below the other, the upper edge of a basal perronate sheath); lamellae strongly decurrent ....
...... **Catathelasma** (298)
(Biannularia)

1. Annulus single; lamellae adnexed to emarginate, not decurrent ......
...... **Armillaria** (299)
(Floccularia)

Tribe Clitocybeae

1. Basidiocarps luminescent; spore print pale drab; spores globose, very large (14-17um) (Japan) .... **Lampteromyces** (232)

1. Basidiocarps not with the above set of features 2

2. Spores amyloid .... **Fayodia** (404)

2. Spores inamyloid 3

3. Pileal surface hymeniform and basidiocarps not associated with termite nests .... **Clitocybe** (234)

3. Pileal surface not hymeniform or if so then associated with termite nests 4

4. Clamps absent 5

4. Clamps present 17

5. Pileus viscid .... **Tricholoma** (251)

5. Pileus not viscid 6

6. Black rhizomorphs present; partial veil forming a distinct annulus; lamellae decurrent; lamellar trama bilateral and with broad hymenpodium .... **Armillariella** (259)

6. Not with the above combination of characteristics 7

7. Lamellae definitely decurrent 8

7. Lamellae not decurrent 13

8. Stipe and pileus arthrospore-bearing (subtropical in South America) .... **Arthrosporella** (262)

8. Stipe and pileus not arthrospore-bearing 9

9. Pileipellis a trichodermium .... **Lulesia** (262)

9. Pileipellis not a trichodermium 10

10. Basidiocarps exuding a latex where cut (tropical fungi; if boreal species see tribe Myceneae) .... **Lactocollybia** (272)

10. Not exuding latex where cut 11

11. Gloeocystidia present .... **Lactocollybia** (272)

11. Gloeocystidia absent 12

12. Pigment incrusting the hyphae of the pileal surface, or hyphae with a membrana pigment; pigments never conspicuously orange and never completely lacking; cystidia absent; lamellar trama not parallel .... **Omphalina** (263)

12. Pigment intracellular, and sometimes conspicuously orange, or pigments lacking altogether (mostly tropical species except the orange ones); cystidia present, lamellar trama parallel .... **Gerronema** (265)

13(6). Basidiocarps associated with termite nests; spore print pink .. 14

13. Basidiocarps and/or spores otherwise 15

14. Pileipellis a cutis; stipe without a pseudorhiza .. **Podobrella** (276)

14. Pileipellis a derm; stipe with a pseudorhiza . **Termitomyces** (277)

15(13). Habit tricholmatoid .... **Tricholoma** (251)

15. Habit pleurotoid or rarely collybioid 16

82

16. Habitat pleurotoid or rarely collybioid; spores and trama hyphae without a purplish red necropigment .... **Pleurocollybia** (274)

16. Habitat collybioid; spores and trama hyphae with a red necropigment .... **Callistosporium** (270)

17(4). Spores ornamented 18

17. Spores smooth 21

18. Having at least one of the following features:
    a) spores with endosporial spinules imbedded in the exosporium;
    b) pleurocystidia present .... **Fayodia** (404)

18. Not having either of the features listed above 19

19. Spore print pink .... **Lepista** (245)

19. Spore print white 20

20. Lamellae thick, subdistant, with broad, regular (parallel) trama, rose-colored or purple; spores globose to short-oval, more than 6um in longest diameter .... **Laccaria** (230)

20. Lamellae thin, close to crowded, not rose-colored or purple; spores ellipsoidal, 4-6um in longest diameter .... **Clitocybe** (234)

21(17). Base of the stipe with a large, flat-margined bulb; partial veil a cortina (Basidiocarps having much the appearance of those of **Cortinarius** subgenus Bulbopodium .... **Leucocortinarius** (624)

21. Base of stipe bulbous or not, but partial veil, if present, not a cortina 22

22. Basidiocarps lignicolous 23

22. Basidiocarps terrestrial 29

23. Edge of lamellae completely heteromorphous from abundant cheilocystidia that are usually conspicuous, well differentiated and very large .... **Tricholomopsis** (249)

23. Edge of lamellae and cheilocystidia not as above 24

24. Habit Clitocyboid; basidiocarps large, fleshy, with thick stipe and deeply decurrent lamellae, bright orange, and luminescent ....
...... **Omphalotus** (232)

24. Basidiocarps not as above 25

25. Habit Omphalinoid 10

25. Habit otherwise 26

  26. Large cystidia with bulbous base and acuminate apex present as pleurocystidia, cheilocystidia, pileocystidia and caulocystidia ......
      ...... **Macrocystidia** (273)

  26. Cystidia, if present, not as above 27

27. Cheilocystidia absent 28

27. Cheilocystia present .... **Pleurocollybia** (274)

  28. Pigment none or merely pale ochraceous; habit Tricholomatoid or Cliocyboid .... **Hypsizygus** (248)

  28. Pigments brown fuscous, beige or pinkish cinnamon; habit pleurotoid or collyboid .... **Plerocollybia** (274)

29(22). Edge of lamellae completely heteromorphous from abundant cheilocystidia that are usually conspicuous and well differentiated ...
     ..... **Tricholomopsis** (249)

29. Edge of lamellae not heteromorphous; Cheilocystidia absent, or few and inconspicuous if present 30

  30. Stipe base arising from a cylidrical, jug-like, or fusoid basal "sclerotium" whose upper margin bears a volva-like rim, or a series of squarrae .... **Squamanita** (480)
    (now in the Cystodermateae)

  30. Stipe not arising from a basal "sclerotium" 31

31. Spores cylindrical or capsule-shaped, 16-22 x 6-9um, lamellae thick, subdistant, purple or lilac; basidiocarps growing only in sand ....
     ...... **Laccaria** (230)

31. Not with the above combination of characteristics 32

  32. Lamellae decurrent (habit Clitocyboid or Omphalinoid) 33

  32. Lamellae sinuate, emarginate, or adnate, but never decurrent (habit Tricholmatoid) 35

33. Lamellar trama interwoven 34

33. Lamellar trama parallel or subparallel 10

34. Having at least one of the following features:
   a) pleurocystidia, caulocystidia, or pileocystidia present,
   b) pileus less than 2cm in diameter, stipe 0.5-2.0mm thick;
   c) orange intracellular or interstitial pigment present . . . .
                  . . . . . **Gerronema** (265)

34. Not having any of the features listed above . . . . . . **Clitocybe** (234)

35(32). Cystidia large, with a bulbous base and acuminate apex, present as cheilocystidia, pleurocystidia, pileocystidia and caulocystidia; habit Collybioid or Mycenoid . . . . **Macrocystidia** (273)

35. Cystidia, if present, not as above; habit rarely Collybioid 36

36. Laticiferous hyphae and/or gloeocystidia present . . . .
                  . . . . . **Lactocollybia** (272)

36. Laticiferous hyphae and gloeocystidia absent 37

37. Habit Tricholomatoid . . . . **Tricholoma** (251)

37. Habit pleurotoid and lignicolous or rarely Collybioid and then humicolous (tropical or subtropical species) . . . . **Pleurocollybia** (274)

Tribe Collybieae

1. Lamellae black or nearly so even in fresh specimens; basidia and hyphae with carbonous granules of a black pigment that becomes blue green in akali (KOH, NH_4OH) staining the tissue blue green . . . .
                  . . . . . . **Anthracophyllum** (307)

1. Lamellae not black (but they may be slate grey); basidia and hyphae lacking black pigment granules that become blue green in akali 2

2. Lamellae venose, very much crisped and anastomosing in an irregular, somewhat reticulate manner . . . . **Plicatura**
         (sometimes placed in the Cantharellaceae or Meruliaceae)

2. Lamellae not venose, crisped nor anastomosing . . . . , 3

3. Habit Pleurotoid with an excentric stipe or with a pseudostipe 4

3. Habit Collybioid or Clitocyboid 5

4. Cheilocystidia filamentous . . . . **Cheimonophyllum** (306)

4. Cheilocystidia not filamentous . . . . **Nothopanus** (304)

5(3). Pileus surface with rameales-structure (i.e. diverticulate hyphae)
...... 6

5. Pileus surface not with rameales-structure, consisting of more or less of smooth, non-diverticulate hyphae 7

    6. Lamellae deeply decurrent; stipe with distinct basal mycelium or with a basal tomentum and arising from a mycelial mat, never truly insititious (tropical or subtropical) .... **Neoclitocybe** (313)

    6. Lamellae subfree to almost decurrent but not deeply decurrent; stipe always insititious .... **Marasmiellus** (315)

7(5). Lamellae deeply decurrent .... **Neoclitocybe** (313)

7. Lamellae not deeply decurrent 8

    8. Pileal surface a viscid pellicle, with numerous imbedded brown pileocystidia; stipe densely velvety; basidiocarps lignicolous ....
...... **Flammulina** (considered a **Pholiota** by Singer)

    8. Not having the above combination of features 9

9. Either the pileal surface is a gelatinized (but not viscid) layer or the stipe arises from or is accompanied by black rhizomorphs ....
...... **Micromphale** (322)

9. Basidiocarps not as above 10

    10. Base of the stipe insititious .... **Marasmiellus** (315)

    10. Base of stipe not insititious, always with a strongly developed basal mycelium .... **Collybia** (308)

Tribe Cystodermateae

1. Pileipellis an epithelium .... **Cystoderma** (478)

1. Pileipellis a trichodermium, a cutis, or hymeniform 2

    2. Spores spinose or echinulate (subtropical or tropical fungi) ....
...... **Ripartitella** (483)

    2. Spores smooth 3

3. Stipitipellis with sphaerocytes .... **Dissoderma** (479)

3. Stipitipellis without sphaerocytes .... **Squamanita** (480)

Note: This tribe is included in the Agaricaceae in Singer's system.

Tribe Leucopaxilleae

1. Spores ornamented (punctate-rough to verruculose or spinulose) .. 2
1. Spores smooth 3

   2. Clamps present; suprahilar plage lacking; pleurocystidia lacking . . . . **Leucopaxillus** (291)

   2. Clamps absent; suprahilar plage present; pleurocystidia or cheilocystidia, or both, often (but not always) present . . . . **Melanoleuca** (294)

3(1). Clamps present 4
3(1). Clamps absent . . . . **Pseudoclitocybe** (287)

   4. Lamellae decurrent, repeatedly dichotomously forked 5
   4. Lamellae not decurrent, or if so, then not repeatedly dichotomously forked 6

5. Spores dextrinoid; lamellar trama bilateral, with broad hymenopodium . . . . **Hygrophoropsis** (688)
5. Spores amyloid; lamellar trama subparallel to interwoven, not bilateral, without a broad hymenopodium . . . . **Cantharellula** (284)

   6(4). Sporocarps lignicolous 7
   6. Sporocarps terrestrial 8

7. Spores elongate, oblong-ellipsoid; cuticular hyphae with incrusting pigment . . . . **Pseudoarmillariella** (285)
7. Spores globose to short-ellipsoid; cuticular hyphae lacking incrusting pigment . . . . **Clitocybula** (288)

   8(6). Cheilocystidia abundant, the lamellar edge heteromorphous; habit tricholomoid . . . . **Porpolma** (290)

   8. Cheilocystidia absent, or few and scattered, the lamellar edge mostly or entirely fertile; habit Omphaloid or Clitocyboid 9

9(8). Sporocarps large to massive, with Clitocyboid habit; spores only slightly amyloid . . . . **Leucopaxillus** (291)
9. Sporocarps small, slender, with Omphaloid habit; spores strongly amyloid . . . . **Pseudoomphalina** (286)

Tribe Lyophylleae

1. Parasitic on other agarics (usually **Russula**); pileal context becoming transformed into a dusty mass of chlamydospores; lamellae reduced, venose, or sometimes absent altogether .... **Asterophora** (224)

1. Not parasitic on other agarics; pileal context not becoming transformed into a powdery mass of chlamydospores; lamellae normal .. 2

   2. Pileal surface cellular .... **Calocybe** (223)

   2. Pileal surface not cellular 3

3. Pigments dull colored (gray, fuscous, umber), or lacking 4

3. Pigment bright colored (yellow, pink, lavender, violet, red, etc.) .....
   ...... **Calocybe** (223)

   4. Pigments absent (sporocarps entirely white) 5

   4. Pigments present, gray or fuscous or brown .... **Lyophyllum** (218)

5. Spores large, smooth; basidia large .... **Lyophyllum** (218)

5. Spores either echinulate, or small and smooth; basidia small ....
   ...... **Calocybe** (223)

Tribe Marasmieae

1. Pileipellis of brooms cells or hymeniform 2

1. Pileal surface not hymeniform nor composed of broom cells but covered with long thick walled dextrinoid hairs 6

   2. Pileipellis consisting of broom cells .... **Marasmius** (350)

   2. Pileipellis not as above 3

3. Pileus tramal hyphae pseudoamyloid .... **Marasmius** (350)

3. Pileus tramal hyphae inamyloid 4

   4. Basidiocarps with the following combination of features;
      a) Clamp connectons present;
      b) Stipe not long radicating;
      c) Pileus glabrous and moist to dry, but not glutinous nor hairy ...
         ...... **Marasmius** (350)

   4. Basidiocarps not with the above combination of features 5

5. Clamp connections present; pileus glutinous; stipe long radicating ...
...... **Oudemansiella** (344)

5. Clamp connections absent; pileus never glutinous; stipe not long radicating .... **Strobilurus** (349)

    6. Stipe present, central or excentric .... **Crinipellis** (368)

    6. Stipe absent or if present, it is rudimentary and is not attached to the substratum .... **Chaetocalathus** (371)

Note: Excludes **Mycenella** which is placed with **Mycena** in the tribe Myceneae.

Tribe Myceneae

1. Hymenophore poroid (mostly tropical species) .... **Filoboletus**

1. Hymenophore lamellate 2

    2. Spores strongly falsely echinulate .... **Fayodia** (404)
(Subgenus **Fayodia**)

    2. Spores not strongly falsely echinulate 3

3. Spores amyloid 4

3. Spores inamyloid 11

    4. Basidiocarps very small and fragile, with membranous, translucent pileal context, venose or very narrow and distant lamellae and no pigments in any part of the basidiocarp .... **Delicatula** (383)

    4. Not with the above combination of characteristics 5

5. Pileus surface viscid to glutinous 6

5. Pileus surface not viscid 7

    6. Spores cyanophilic (at least in part) .... **Myxomphalia** (404)

    6. Spores acyanophilic .... **Mycena** (380, 384, 397)

7(5). Base of stipe with a tuft of tawny or ferruginous tomentum; all hyphae inamyloid .... **Xeromphalina** (407)

7. Not with the above combination of characteristics 8

8. Lignicolous or with a pseudorhiza on conifer cones . . . .
. . . . . . **Baeospora** (409)

8. Humicolous (may be on woody humus but not lignicolous) 9

9. Pileipellis cellular or hymeniform; pileal tramal hyphae inamyloid; cystidia absent . . . . **Dermoloma** (402)

9. Basidiocarp not with the above combination of features 10

    10. Collybioid to almost Tricholomatoid with narrowly adnexed or deeply sinuate lamellae; stipe stuffed or solid (a tropical genus) . . .
    . . . . . . **Dennisomyces** (401)

    10. Mostly Omphalinoid or Mycenoid, if Collybioid or Tricholomatoid the stipe is not stuffed nor solid . . . . **Mycena** (380, 384, 397)

11(3). Phaeocystidia present . . . . **Fayodia** (404)

11. Phaeocystidia absent 12

    12. Pileus cellular or hymeniform; pileus trama inamyloid; cystidia absent . . . . **Dermoloma** (402)

    12. Basidiocarp not with the above combination of features 13

13. Spores cyanophilic (at least in part) . . . . **Fayodia** (404)
(subgenus **Heterosporula**)

13. Spores acyanophilic . . . . **Mycena** (380, 384, 397)

.

Tribe Panelleae

1. Hymenophore poroid . . . . **Dictyopanus** (338)

1. Hymenophore lamellate 2

    2. Spores weakly or indistinctly amyloid, or seemingly inamyloid; sporocarp sessile; pellicular veil present . . . . **Tectella** (337)

    2. Spores strongly (or at least distinctly) amyloid; sporocarp variously attached, not lacking a pellicular veil . . . . **Panellus** (339)

Tribe Pseudohiatuleae

1. Pileus surface a viscid pellicle .... **Flammulina** (413)
1. Pileus surface not viscid 2

  2. Dermatocystidia conspicuously thick-walled 3
  2. Dermatocystidia either thin-walled or inconsistently thickened .. 5

3. Spores amyloid .... **Pseudohiatula** (415)
3. Spores inamyloid 4

  4. Lateral strata of lamellae gelatinized .... **Pseudohiatula** (415)
  4. Lateral strata of lamellae not or weakly gelatinized (omit area near gill edge) .... **Cyptotrama** (416)

5(2). Hymenophoral trama decidedly bilateral; lamellae distant to sub-distant .... **Cyptotrama** (416)
5. Hymenophoral trama weakly and indistinctly bilateral; lamellae close to subclose .... **Flammulina** (413)

Tribe Resupinateae

1. Conspicuous, thick walled metuloids present ... **Hohenbuehelia** (332)
1. Metuloids absent (cheilocystidia may be present) . **Resupinatus** (330)

Tribe Rhodoteae

1. Basidiocarps always associated with termite nests; spore print pink spores smooth; clamps absent (tropical fungi) ... **Termitomyces** (277)
1. Basidiocarps lignicolous, with tough-gelatinous pileal surface in which are imbedded the pedicels of a hymeniform layer of vesiculose, thick walled ampullaceous cells; spore print creamy pink; spores echinulate
      ...... **Rhodotus** (418)

INDEX